4-22-63   60-148739   spares

Well, Mary

CIVIL WAR LETTERS

OF A

WISCONSIN VOLUNTEER

Well Mary

CIVIL WAR LETTERS

OF A WISCONSIN VOLUNTEER

Edited by Margaret Brobst Roth

The University of Wisconsin Press

Madison, 1960

Published by The University of Wisconsin Press
430 Sterling Court, Madison 6, Wisconsin

Copyright © 1960 by the Regents of the University of Wisconsin

Printed in the United States of America by the
George Banta Company, Inc., Menasha, Wisconsin
Library of Congress Catalog Card Number 60-14839

Acknowledgments

For their assistance in assembling these letters, I am indebted to my parents. For their help and interest in the project, I would like to thank Miss Dorothea Krause, of the Wausau Public Library, and Miss Josephine Harper, of the Wisconsin Historical Society. For preparing the maps for my book, I am grateful to the Cartographic Laboratory, Department of Geography, University of Wisconsin. And the entire job was made lighter by words of encouragement from Mr. William Hesseltine, Mr. August Derleth, and Mr. Bruce Catton, who each felt the letters were worthy of our efforts.

M. B. R.

Wausau, Wisconsin
November, 1959

Contents

Illustrations and Maps

Well, Mary

CIVIL WAR LETTERS
OF A
WISCONSIN VOLUNTEER

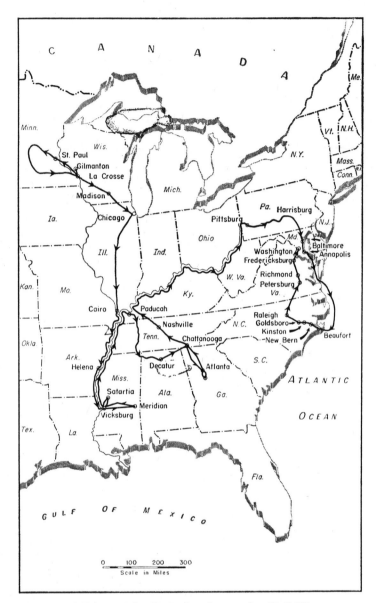

Itinerary of Private John F. Brobst during the Civil War

Introduction

The letters of Private John F. Brobst of the Twenty-fifth Wisconsin Infantry Regiment are reproduced here for the first time. John served with the Union Army for nearly three years during the Civil War. At Vicksburg his regiment was a part of Montgomery's Brigade, Kimball's Division, Sixteenth Army Corps (General Washburn), Army of the Tennessee, under General Ulysses S. Grant. John later served with General William T. Sherman in the Meridian and Atlanta campaigns, his regiment being in the Second Brigade, Fourth Division (Generals Veatch and Fuller), Sixteenth Army Corps (General Dodge), Army of the Tennessee, under General James B. McPherson. During the winter of 1864–65, John was separated from his regiment and served with General T. F. Meagher's Provisional Division near Chattanooga. He later rejoined his regiment in North Carolina, and marched to Washington, D.C., with the Second Brigade, First Division, Seventeenth Army Corps (General Blair), Army of the Tennessee, under General O. O. Howard.

John's letters may be no more remarkable than hundreds of other Civil War letters, but they are unique in one respect—they have not been exposed to the thorough scrutiny of family, friends, and scholars which has been given to other letters and diaries written by Civil War soldiers. The letters which are printed here were kept by their recipient, Mary Englesby, for more than seventy years, during which time no one else read them. The letters had meant a lot to Mary. They had been written to her when she was in her early teens, by a young soldier who was a friend of the family. The first letters he had written were the kind she could share with her father and mother, but later ones became more personal. As time passed and the correspondence between John and Mary continued, they came to know and respect each other as never before. By the time John had returned home in 1865, he and Mary were engaged to be married. Time and separation had, in their case, served to strengthen their relationship rather than strain it. The letters John had written were treasured by Mary as her love letters, and for that reason she had kept them to herself for so many years.

After Mary's death in 1943, the letters lay forgotten in a

box of her belongings, until an unusual circumstance led to a search for them. My parents, Mr. and Mrs. W. E. Brobst, had just moved into their home on Lathrop Street in Madison, Wisconsin, when they noticed a large metal manhole cover in the middle of their driveway. After consulting neighbors and city maps, they found out that the manhole cover enclosed what once was a cistern providing water for Civil War troops stationed at nearby Camp Randall. Remembering that my great-grandfather had been stationed at Camp Randall for some time, and had told some entertaining stories about his experiences there, my parents decided to try to locate the letters he had written while he served in the Civil War. Mother recalled that great-grandma kept the letters in a box and occasionally took them out to read them over again. But where the letters had gone after her death was a mystery to us. After making some apparently fruitless inquiries among the relatives, it seemed that the letters had simply disappeared. Then an aunt in Schenectady, New York, Mrs. J. E. Brobst, found them in a small box tucked away in a bookcase and sent them on to my parents.

The letters were soon thereafter microfilmed by the Wisconsin Historical Society at Madison. After other members of the family had read them and agreed that an effort should be made to have them published, we began the job of organizing them for publication. It has been an interesting project for all of us, and in the process we have learned much about the Civil War and the men who fought in it.

The letters of Private John Brobst substantiate much of the information already published regarding the people he encountered and the battles he fought. But some of the ideas and opinions he expresses are enlightening, especially since his individual opinions were undoubtedly shared by thousands of his fellow soldiers in the Union Army.

In addition to the accounts of marches and battles and military things that make John's letters interesting, we find a love story gradually emerging as the central theme around which John built his hopes and dreams. He was a different kind of person in many ways by the end of the war.

Some of the letters John wrote are now missing, and others are fragmentary, but those which remain have been included here in their entirety, except one passage as noted. For the sake of readability, the capitalization, punctuation, grammar, and spelling of the original letters have been somewhat modified; otherwise the words and sentence structure are John Brobst's and preserve the original flavor of his style. John signed his name "Brobest" in some of the letters, probably perpetuating a mistake made when he was mustered in. He dropped the "e" when he came home. The usual form of the name, "Brobst," is used here.

No attempt has been made to include an explanation of every phase of the Civil War, but it did seem necessary to provide some background information at the beginning of each chapter in order to establish the relationship between John's activities and those of the troops with which he was serving. Footnotes have been used occasionally to clarify certain details regarding individuals or places. But for the most part the letters are clear in meaning, and they required no embellishment to make them enjoyable reading.

CHAPTER ONE

March 1863–July 1863

"It will soon be over"

The young volunteers of the Twenty-fifth Wisconsin Infantry Regiment had arrived at last in the land of Dixie. They were all in high spirits, having waited impatiently for many long months to be sent here. The South was bustling with wartime activity, and the whole adventure promised much in the way of excitement. At the moment, they could not imagine the many hardships which lay ahead, as the war was not expected to last very long.

As they looked down on the Mississippi River from high

on the bluffs at Columbus, Kentucky, these young men
from Wisconsin could witness the spectacle of thousands
of men and tremendous quantities of supplies, artillery
and ammunition being shipped downstream toward the
front lines. It was a thrill to be so close to the fighting, and
they felt sure that their regiment would soon be on its way
to battle. Meanwhile there was the usual drilling and
picket duty to perform, while they waited for orders to
move.

This new Wisconsin regiment had yet to see any real
action, having been organized just a few months previ-
ously. There had been a call for volunteers in August of
1862, when the government in Washington had finally
realized that the rebellion of the South would not be easily
quelled. If the quota of recruits for Wisconsin could not
be filled by volunteers, they would have to resort to the
draft, which was considered a shameful way to raise
troops. Recruiting officers had been sent around the state,
and enough men had signed up to form several new regiments. Recruits were assured of being able to serve with
their friends and neighbors if they signed up together.

The Twenty-fifth Wisconsin, one of the new regiments,
had been recruited mainly from the western counties of
the state, Company G being made up of soldiers from
Buffalo County. Among them were six boys from Gilmanton, a small frontier farm community near the Mississippi
River. These six volunteers, John Brobst, John Christian,
Chauncey Cooke;[1] Dan Hadley, Phil Knowles, Thompson
Pratt, and Wallace Wilcox, were destined to spend the
following three years living, marching, and fighting together, learning the new and hazardous job of soldiering

[1] See Cooke, in *Wisconsin Magazine of History,* IV and V.

in the infantry. All but one would return home at the end
of the Civil War, having survived the most bloody conflict
known to their world.

John Brobst was typical of these young soldiers. He was
in his early twenties and unmarried, as were most of the
men in his company. He was of medium height and stocky
build, and appeared capable of handling any task involv-
ing physical strength. John had felt that it was his duty to
volunteer for service. His stand on the question of abolition was undecided, but he did think it would be a disgrace to allow the rebellious southern states to secede.

In September of 1862, John Brobst and his friends had
been mustered in at La Crosse, Wisconsin, as privates in
the Twenty-fifth Wisconsin Regiment. There they drilled
for a few short weeks, and left for Minnesota to put down
a sudden Sioux uprising, which had subsided by the time
they arrived. The regiment was then divided, and the
companies scattered around the state to prevent a recur-
rence of the revolt. This particular assignment was not a
popular one, as most of these volunteers felt they had enlisted to fight rebs, not redskins.

Actually, the Indians were the least of their troubles in
Minnesota. The casualties they suffered there were not
due to battle wounds, but were rather the result of a serious epidemic of measles which hit the regiment in November. These seemingly rugged young frontiersmen had ex-
perienced hardships and dangers in their home state of
Wisconsin, but many of them had never been exposed to
the most common contagious diseases.[2]

As the Indian scare in Minnesota dissolved, the Twenty-
fifth Wisconsin had begun the long march back home, a

[2] See Wiley, *The Life of Billy Yank,* p. 133.

distance of nearly three hundred miles through the cold
north country on extremely poor roads. By the middle of
December, the Twenty-fifth had finally reached La
Crosse. A few days later they left by rail for Camp Randall
at Madison for training.

This was the first train ride for many of the men, and a
thrilling experience, but they found little to please them in
Madison. Here they spent hours drilling out in the cold
every day, living in converted cow barns and eating sour
bread and spoiled beef.[3] They managed to get into trouble
with their officers and the local police in their spare time.
These young woodsmen and farmers did not take to army
rank or discipline, and wanted to come and go as they
pleased. They felt that all this training was a waste of time
when there was a war to be fought. After four months of
service, the regiment still looked more like backwoodsmen
than soldiers. The men were not only indifferent to their
non-military appearance, but loudly expressed their con-
tempt for the polish and elegant dress of the eastern
troops.

For the most part, the men of the Twenty-fifth enjoyed
nothing more than a good joke or a good fight. One of the
Gilmanton boys, Thompson Pratt, had spent his last two
weeks at Camp Randall in hiding, with his friends bringing him food after dark. The trouble began during one of
the endless drill sessions. Tom, who was naturally stoop-
shouldered, had lost his temper when a drill sergeant
poked him in the back and yelled, "Straighten up, soldier!"
Tom had turned and swung; he caught the unsuspecting

[3] See Roesch, "Memorandum," pp. 3–4.

sergeant square on the chin and knocked him out. It might have meant a court-martial for Tom if he had been caught, but he had managed to stay out of sight until the Twenty-fifth was ready to leave Madison; by that time the search for him had been abandoned.

On February 17, 1863, the Twenty-fifth Wisconsin Regiment had left its home state for the second time, this time to travel south. The order to leave Camp Randall was a welcome one, and the Wisconsin soldiers were certain they would soon be joining General Grant, in his campaign to take Vicksburg, Mississippi. They had no way of knowing that two more months of drilling and marking time awaited them in Columbus, Kentucky, where troops and supplies were being massed in preparation for the attempt to take Vicksburg.

There was boredom and monotony at Columbus, and living conditions of the camp became increasingly worse. As the weather grew warmer, more and more of the men became ill, and yet nothing was done to improve the unsanitary state of the camp. Tents were pitched much too close together, refuse and garbage littered the open ground, and latrines were simply ditches at the edge of the camp area. Rations consisted of hardtack, coffee, and pork, cooked over individual campfires. Drinking water was contaminated more often than not, and these northerners failed to realize that even spring water was not always safe to drink.[4]

Soon other Wisconsin regiments began to arrive, and many friends from home were greeted warmly. The

[4] See Wiley, *The Life of Billy Yank,* pp. 126–27.

morale of the men in the Twenty-fifth was remarkably
high, considering their unhealthy living conditions. There
were songs and horseplay in camp, with an occasional
card game or an attempt at baseball. At least they were
given a measure of freedom here, and when not on duty,
John Brobst and his Wisconsin friends explored the countryside. They picked blackberries and debated the Union
cause with the southerners and with each other. They met
"darkies" for the first time and took sides on the question
of abolition. And they became increasingly convinced of
the righteousness of the cause for which they were about
to fight.

During the long and lonely hours of picket duty, John
Brobst would think of home and wonder when, if ever, he
would again return to Wisconsin, to a farm of his own.
The only time the Gilmanton recruits had been home
since their enlistment was in December when they had
been given a few days' furlough after their Minnesota expedition. They had all been treated like heroes, although
none of them had even seen a reb as yet. There had been
a dance at the mill, and John had enjoyed the attention he
received, especially from Elsie Hammond, his favorite
among the local girls. The only trouble was, she seemed to
like all the other boys just as well. John had stayed over-
night with Elsie's family before leaving for La Crosse, and
it seemed to him that Elsie did not make as big a fuss
about him as the rest of her family did. Elsie's niece, Mary
Englesby, had asked him to write to her, and promised
some letters in return. Mary was only thirteen, but she was
a cheerful, vivacious girl, and would probably be a more
dependable letter writer than Elsie. John needed someone

to write to, as he no longer felt close to his own family. His mother had died when he was young, back in Ohio, and he had come to Wisconsin with the Allens. John still heard from his brother and sisters occasionally, but after years of separation their correspondence had dwindled.

Letter writing had become a common pastime among the troops at camp, but for most of them it was a difficult undertaking. Their formal education had been neglected, as schools and teachers were scarce along the frontier. For many, learning to read the family Bible had been a real accomplishment. But they felt the effort involved in writing letters was worthwhile, as it was sure to bring news of home in return. There was no restriction as to what they could write about; the only censorship they encountered was their own lack of vocabulary or writing materials.

It was to Mary Englesby that John wrote, one spring day in 1863, hoping to hear some precious news of home. Not long afterward, her answer arrived, initiating a correspondence which continued throughout the Civil War.

John's letters contained numerous inaccuracies due to the common tendency among soldiers to exaggerate numbers of troops and losses. His sincerity and humor, however, are very much in evidence as he records his impressions of a war that was anything but amusing. His letters often demonstrate how a soldier's outlook can waver between bravado and disillusionment, depending upon the state of his health and the course of the war. They portray John as a young man in the process of finding himself, and they reveal a gradual change in his feeling toward Mary, the girl at home.

14   *Chapter* i

[Columbus, Kentucky]

[Beginning of letter missing.]

Times are as dull here as they can be up there. There is
nothing going on here but the one thing over and over
again, but we pass away the time by playing tricks on
each other, do anything for excitement. We are not
penned up like a pack of hogs as we were at Madison.[5]

The general says give men what liberty they can, and
then the men will be ashamed to try and run away, and
it is about so.

We get an excuse from the Captain and go where we
have a mind to. I went out in the country before I was
sick and had more fun than I have had for some time. The
ladies are all secesh,[6] so are the men for that matter, but
they dare not talk it, and the ladies dare, so of course I
had to quarrel with all of them that I saw. I told one of
them that the Yankee boys were the best of fellows when
they once got acquainted with them, that there were lots
of girls up north that would tell them so, but they were
hard to get acquainted with, for the Yankees introduced
themselves with gun cartridge and bayonet, and the way
the rebels received them was by turning their heels to-
wards us and throwing dust in our faces, by running to
get away from us. Oh, you had ought to have seen her.
It made her so mad she did not know what to [do]. She
said I would see which side would whip. I told her there
were women enough up north to whip the rebels, but we
did not dare to let them come for they would kill every

[5] Camp Randall, Madison, Wisconsin.
[6] Secessionist.

one of them. She said I was a fool, that she always knew that the Yankees were fools but I was the greatest fool she ever saw, and I came away and left her mad as a wet hen, and have not seen her since, and I suppose she never wants to see me again.

I am glad the settlers are coming in there. I want to see that all settled up there when I get back, for I know I shall be lonesome. I do not want you to think that I like to soldier better than anything that I ever got at, for I do not, but there are so many here all the time, that when one gets to work all alone it will go tough for awhile at first. I think so, at least.

I think they can't change Eagle Bluff[7] so but what I will know that. The more that settles in, the more lively it will be for you that are there.

I wish I could be there to that dance. I think that you will have a good time and I would like to be there with you, but I can't, so there is no use of talking. You must not think because a man is a soldier he enjoys himself better than at home. Home is sweet and friends are dear, but what would they all be to let the country go to ruin, and be a slave. I am contented with my lot, in one sense of the word, for I know that I am doing my duty, and I know that it is my duty to do as I am now a-doing. If I live to get back, I shall be proud of the freedom I shall have, and know that I helped to gain that freedom. If I should not get back, it will do them good that do get back.

We have three fiddles in our company. Dan[8] is trying to

[7] Eagle Peak, near Gilmanton, Wisconsin.

[8] Private Daniel R. Hadley, Gilmanton, Wisconsin, Company G. 25th Wisconsin Infantry Regiment. Dan is mentioned often, perhaps because Mary inquired about him.

learn to play on a fiddle. He has sawed about two weeks and can't play a tune. He is busy as a nailer at it now. I make him mad at me sometimes laughing at him, but he soon gets over it. Thompson Pratt[9] has got a little nigger to wait on him. He gives him three dollars per month. He is running opposition to the Captain's. He sits in his tent and sends the darky to the cook shanty to get fire to light his pipe, and has him sweep out the tent, bring water to wash and drink.

In fact he has the darky on the jump all of the time. Thompson takes comfort. He does not send hardly any money home, so he has plenty of money with him all the time and just enjoys himself, and I do not know but what that is about as good a way as any, but if he was to get wounded he would wish he had sent his money home. I tell him so, but he says this world owes him a living and he will have it at all events.

The Twenty-seventh Wis. Regt. is here. There are lots of boys in it from Sheboygan that I know, and when I get tired of staying here, I go over there and gas awhile for pastime. [*Rest of letter missing.*]

> Headquarters 2d Brigade. 15th Division
> 16th Army Corps, Camped on
> Reeds Bluff, Miss.
> June the 18th, A.D./63

Dear Friend Mary,

I received your welcome letter yesterday. Was glad to

[9] Corporal Thompson L. Pratt, Gilmanton, Wisconsin, Company G, 25th Wisconsin Infantry Regiment.

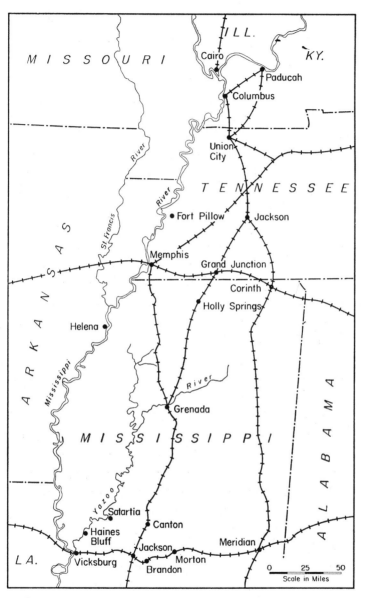

In the Mississippi Valley

hear from you and to hear that you are well. I am well and
hearty as can be.

We have had a long journey since I wrote to you last,
and some of the way it was a very hard one. We took the
boat at Columbus and came down the Miss. River to the
Yazoo River and from there up to Satartia. There we had
a very little fun with the rebels. They did not stand to
fight us much. There were some troops went in ahead of
us, and when they saw us a-coming they ran for life, but
we took fifty prisoners and only lost one man killed on our
side, and he was out of the 8th Wis., and took about 75
head of beef cattle, 100 mules, a large amount of cotton.
About 700 slaves came with us. We burned the town, and
the rebel Johnston[10] made his appearance with 40,000 men
and we had only 4,000. We had to retreat back to Haines
Bluff, but he did not attack us on our retreat. We stayed
at Haines Bluff three days when orders came to march
away, when we came here. We are now three miles from
Vicksburg on the reserve. We have had no stand up and
fight yet, but expect one every day. The rebels want to
get into Vicksburg to help those that are there, but I do
not think they can. They will have to fight to get there, at
all events. There are 250,000 men here under Grant's[11]
command, but some of them are 40 miles apart, but there
are 25,000 here where Johnston will have to come to get to
Vicksburg. I must stop writing to dine, take my chunk of
hard bread and meat.

Well, dinner is over and I feel some better. It is a very
stirring time here. While I have been writing to you there
were 13 rebels came in and gave themselves up. They are

[10] General Joseph E. Johnston.
[11] General Ulysses S. Grant.

right here in front of my tent. They say they will not fight any longer and have all their property destroyed and get whipped in the end. They are coming in every day more or less. Those that are here say that there are 800 more outside of our lines that have stacked arms and want to come in and give themselves up. The cavalry has gone out after them to bring them in. It may prove false, but I think it is true for I do not think they would tell it if it was not true.

They are deserting out of Vicksburg all the time. There were 28 came in yesterday. They say there are 4,000 in there that have laid down their arms and say they are whipped and will not fight any more. I can sit here and hear the guns firing and see the shells bust over Vicksburg. Grant gives them three hours every day to bury their dead and take care of their wounded. They can't go near their guns without our sharpshooters picking them off, so they cannot hurt our men in the least. Grant gave them ten days to get their women and children out of the place, but they would not take them out in that time, but let it run over four days and then sent them out, and Grant sent them back and told them the day of reckoning had come and they were too late. So they had to go back and stay there. I think it served them right. Learn them to take a joke. Those copperheads that are so afraid up there have no cause to be so, for I do not think they ever will be needed in this war for I think it will soon be over, and we will all be at home to tend to them.

I think you are safe from being cut out now, for there are no girls here. They have all left and gone with the secesh, but as the darkies say, I am done gone. I think I should like you for a niece very well. I think you would be a good one. Too bad for Elsie. Hope she will soon get well, but she had no business to give me the mitten then. I would not have had her have that fever.

You say strawberries are getting ripe up there. Blackberries are ripe here and apples, peaches, [and] plums are ripe. Most all kinds of fruit are ripe here now, but it is most dreadful hot weather here. There were 17 men here sun struck in one day's march out of our brigade. We have to work every other day building fortifications and that is all that we have to do, and we are willing to do that to save our scalps. There is policy in war as well as all other things, you know. One scalp saved is worth two that are not saved. [*Rest of letter missing.*]

Headquarters 2d Brigade
16th Army Corps
Camped in rear of
Vicksburg
July the 5th/63

Friend Mary,

I now seat myself to let you all know what kind of a Fourth we had. You folks up there had a more sociable time, perhaps, than we had, but I know you could not be half as happy as we were. We had the unspeakable pleasure of planting our glorious old flag in Vicksburg at four o'clock on the morning of the Fourth. There was pleasure and the right kind of pleasure. At 4 o'clock in the morning of the Fourth the rebels took down their flag and ran up a white one that was a surrender. Then they came out on the breastworks and stacked their arms and fell back and our men took possession and went out and took down the white flag, and the stars and stripes, our flag, that floats so proudly over the southern Gibraltar is 36 feet long. It is the greatest victory of the war.

We got twenty-five thousand prisoners and twelve thousand Negroes. The rebels say that when Grant drove them in there they had forty thousand men, and we killed ten thousand and five thousand died. They had no medicines for their sick, and nothing but mule beef to eat for nine days. They are about as glad as we are in two hours after Vicksburg was taken. Grant ordered one hundred thousand men after the rebel Johnston. He has fifty thousand men, and Grant wants to get him surrounded before he hears that Vicksburg is taken. If he succeeds in taking Johnston, we will all be home in three months. I think we have to go after Price.[12] We went after him once but had to come back. We only had 1,000 men and he 7,000 so we had to come back. I have had the pleasure of hearing the balls whistle around my ears a little, but we did not get a man hurt. The rebs lost 5 killed and 7 wounded that we know of. How many more we can't tell. Some of our boys were badly scared. One fell down and thought a horse ran over him, but the most of them have done well. For the first time your little Dan was not with us. He is quite sick or at least he makes an awful fuss. You must take no offense when I call him your little Dan. If folks did not talk they would not say anything. I feel so good over the great victory that I do not know what I am saying half of the time. We go around here yelling like a parcel of Indians. Grant is the only man that can whip the rebs every time, and he can do it every time that he tries it. We would not give

[12] General Sterling Price.

our General Grant for all the generals that are in the northern army. When his men go in a fight they know he is going to have us whip them.

I do not know where we will be by the time that you get this, perhaps five hundred miles from here and fighting some great battle. The 25th has got down here in the field now where they will have plenty of fighting to do and I hope we will do it like men, for the Wisconsin boys are called good fighters.

I have got my picture taken but it is a very poor one, but is the best that I could get.

Our good news was all the Fourth we had, but it made us feel better than we would have felt if we had not got the news. I hope you had a good time there the Fourth and enjoyed yourself. Well, Elsie has soured on me. She has popped me off the handle short as pie crust, and just imagine how I must feel. Dan has cut me out sure. If I get him out of the way you need not think strange of it. You can tell your father[13] the news and save me writing it over. It is very warm here, plenty of all kinds of fruit. I wish you had some of the nice peaches and apples that are here, and pears, in fact, everything. Goodbye for the present.

Write soon direct to Cairo, Ill., Co. G, 2[5]th. You liked them songs. I will send you another.

Yours truly,
from a friend,

John F. Brobst

[13] Mary's father was Harrison Englesby, Gilmanton, Wisconsin.

CHAPTER TWO

November 1863–January 1864

"A dreary lonesome life"

The seige of Vicksburg was over, and on that glorious Fourth of July it looked to Grant's troops as though the war would soon be over too. They would not have believed that two more years of fighting and hardship would be endured before the Confederacy could be forced to surrender. But Vicksburg was an important victory, a turning point in the western campaign. After the fall of Port Hudson a few days later, the entire Mississippi River could be controlled by the Union forces. The outcome of the war was at this point already decided, but few realized the lengths to which the Confederacy would go for the slightest chance of turning the tide.

During that month of July, 1863, in Mississippi, the Twenty-fifth Wisconsin suffered its worst ordeal of illness, as one by one every soldier in the regiment contracted malaria or dysentery. On the twentieth of July, five hundred men lay sick, and not more than one hundred were fit for duty. Malaria was called "the ague," typhoid was "swamp fever," and dysentery "the quickstep"; many of the men were unaware of the causes or nature of their sickness. By the end of the war, the deaths from these diseases would far outnumber the deaths from battle wounds.[1]

In July and August of 1863, the entire regiment was sent up the Mississippi River to Helena, Arkansas, to remain until the following February, being detailed as Provost Guard of the Post.

During the winter months of the Civil War, the fighting often came to a standstill, as long marches and camping in the open were hampered by the slush, rain, and mud of the southern winter. Whenever possible the troops were housed in semipermanent barracks or huts, and were occupied mainly with drilling, in anticipation of the renewed action that would inevitably come with spring weather.

On the western front, many of the Union troops had their winter quarters in towns along the Mississippi River, an important supply route. Helena, Arkansas, was such a town, and it was here that the Twenty-fifth Wisconsin spent the winter of 1863–64. Living conditions for the

---

[1] See Wiley, *The Life of Billy Yank*, p. 124; Campbell, *Wisconsin in Three Centuries*, III, 286.

troops were somewhat improved, and cooler weather brought considerable relief from the sickness which had plagued the regiment all summer. As their health returned, so did the enthusiasm of the boys from Wisconsin, and they willingly went about their tedious routine of picket duty and drilling, with an occasional scouting detail to search for rebs.

Soldiering seemed easier now that they had the hang of it. Although thoughts of home and families were still uppermost in the minds of these volunteers, they were resigned to serving out their three years if necessary. John Brobst and his Gilmanton friends were beginning to realize that the war was not yet won, and that preparations were being made for an extensive campaign in the South in the spring. Meanwhile, they made the most of their leisure time, knowing that they would soon be on the move again.

[Helena, Arkansas
November, 1863]

[Beginning of letter missing.]

I have commenced this letter the 29th of November and shall give you a diary of the many things that transpire every day in camp life as they will no doubt be interesting to you.

I shall commence on the 28th of November as I have just returned from a scout that we had on that day. Orders came at 4 o'clock in the afternoon for fifty men to march with two days rations of provisions and by 5 o'clock we were on the steamer "Cheek" and by daylight next morning we landed opposite island No. 65. There we disembarked and took our course due west. After going some 5 miles we found a camp where there had been some guerrillas but they had gone, so seven of us started in advance of the main body and soon surrounded a plantation. Myself and another one went in to see what they had in the house and we found something very nice. There sat three birds that we call guerrillas. One of them was smoking his pipe. We demanded a surrender immediately. Two of them gave themselves up, the other started off on the run. We sent two messengers of death after him, which soon brought him, too. He fell but was not hit, raised up, raised his hands over his head, a surrender. He said he fell so as not to have us shoot any more. The two balls came too close for comfort.

They had each a double barrel shot gun and each a horse and saddle. These with about 25 chickens were all our prisoners, but we being very cruel and hard-hearted we showed no quarters for the hens, but slaughtered them without mercy. The next that fell in our hands was a steady old cow, who not thinking any harm, was shot down, dressed, and put in the wagon. The next was three very fine hogs who fared a similar fate. Now our time was at an end. We had to go back to the main body and let some others take the advance. They captured 5 prisoners and quite a number of hogs, chickens, geese, turkeys, sweet potatoes, etc. We then came back, re-embarked, and started for camp with 8 prisoners, 11 horses, and 8 shotguns besides our other booty. This ends up this scout. Nothing more passes of any note except camp tricks for several days.

Dec. the 4th. Another call for scouts, one day's rations, the best marksmen in the regt. Something afloat we think. We get ready, now comes a guide. He is a loyal southerner driven inside of our lines. He starts off, we follow him. He soon deploys us in the woods as skirmishers, and now we advance. Presently, we hear a rustling in the leaves, and now we see them surrounded, can't get away, but must surrender—19 guerrillas, the very ones that destroyed our guide's property and drove him in our lines. He has revenge. They are all prisoners of war. Now our fun is played out. We must go back to camp and await the next order.

Dec. the 9th. Here comes the expected call. Another scout, one day's rations, then we are off for some more fun. We go on the steamer "Bell Memphis," and up the river we go to the mouth of the St. Francis River, then up that river. This time I have to stay back and let others have the best of the fun. They hunt all day but find nothing. Our rations all gone but must stay another day without any food, but we will have some in the morning when we find a plantation.

A party of boys have gone ahead. They get all around the first house before they are seen. They find 7 guerrillas in the house waiting for their breakfast. Our boys eat their meal for them and take them prisoners with their horses, and we start back and have landed safe on the banks of the Mississippi at Helena. This tells you all the exploits up to the present time. We will see what more will happen before I hear from you.

Dec. the 16th. Another scout, but I did not go with them.

They had a good time. All here safe but one man in Co. E. He got wounded in the knee but not very severe. They got a number of prisoners.

Dec. the 25th, Christmas Day. Another scout. I am one of the number. We go up the St. Francis River. We have a good time. We kill a nice fat turkey and make a secesh woman cook it. She said she would not do it at first, but we scared her so that she cooked the turkey, and we had a good Christmas. We got 22 prisoners this time, 30 horses and some other things such as we always get, but we had a fine time. I hope you had as good a time. [*Rest of letter missing.*]

[*Beginning of letter missing.*]

I have been taking opium for some time to prepare for the shake[2] and I think with the best of care and plenty of opium I will survive the shake with little or no effect on the brain.

Oh, how I wish the cruel thoughts were over, gone and passed from remembrance, but I have always heard the road of true love was rough, and if we had stayed away from them hills and mountains at Vicksburg the road of my love would have been smooth as glass, but it was always my luck to be led in some scrape and then left to get out the best that I could. Uncle Sam is to blame. He did it all, but I have forgave him all.

So you think that picture does not look natural. Well,

[2] A combination of drugs and quinine was the usual prescription during the Civil War for soldiers suffering from malaria.

I will agree with you there but it was the best that they could take and then I broke two or three machines looking in them to get that picture taken. But I will get a better one taken the first chance I have and send to you. But you must not show it to your aunt, will you.

Well, I wish I was up there to go a hare hunting with your father and uncle, but that will not be until the war is over. I do not think I shall try to go home until I can stay there for good. Tell your father if he don't write to me I shan't chase deer for him when I get back again. A soldier's life is a dreary, lonesome life, yet a stranger might come in camp and see them and go off and think them perfectly happy with their lot, but when they think of home the name is sweet. We live well. We go out and borrow a chicken or two, nights. My partner and me stew them up and have general feasts all to ourselves. My respects to that aunt of yours and all of your folks and yourself. Hoping this will find you all well and the request of an early answer, I will close. Direct to Helena, Ark., and the regt., Co., etc.

Yours truly, goodby for the present from a friend.

JFB/MEE

Helena, Ark., Jan. the 19th/64

Dear respected Friend Mary,

It was with great pleasure that I received your ever-welcome letter and devoured the contents, as a hungry lion devours his prey. I was glad to hear of your good health. My health is good as usual and hope when this comes to hand it will find you still enjoying the same blessing.

Your letter was written before Christmas and New Year so you would not tell me how you did enjoy yourself, but I hope you had a gay and happy time and I wish you a happy New Year all this year and for the next forty to come. I spent my holidays real soldier fashion. Lots of fun, but when I came to sit down and sum it all up it did not amount to but very little. What little it did amount to was just the sum of an 0.

I had written an answer to your letter before I received it, and I guess you will be sick of letters by the time that you get through reading it, for it covers a quarter section of paper, besides some that I have here that it don't cover. If you are fond of long letters and not much news I can supply you very well I think.

William Anderson,[3] the tall slim young man that you danced the polkey with up at the mill, is dead. He died the 22nd of December. He was a good soldier, much loved and respected in the Co. We miss him greatly, but of such is the trials of war, and the clever as well as others must go when it is their unlucky fate.

You say you wish we were all at home. Well, so do I, but we cannot be yet, and not for some time to come. The best prospects are that we will have the pleasure of serving our time out. And then again, if we were to come home, I fear that you would soon get tired of us, for we would be so full of that old gent—I forget what they do call him now, but he is the chief proprietor of that dark

[3] Private William E. Anderson, Durand, Wisconsin, Company G, 25th Wisconsin Infantry Regiment. He died of disease on December 28, 1863, Cairo, Illinois, according to the Wisconsin *Roster*.

region that the preacher tells us about, the one that coaxes the sinners in, then locks the door and loses the key, and leaves the poor sinner in the limbos.

I wish I could have been up there to run and head off the deer for your father when he was out on that hunt of his. I have run so much since I have been in the army that I think I could do better than I did two years ago. But you must not think we run from the rebs. No indeed, I should sacrifice my last relation first but not my sweet self. Brave, am I not?

We have some very cold weather here for this country. Those that live here say that it is very uncommon for this country. There have been several frozen to death here. And it is snowing here today, but the snow is not more than two inches deep, but the mud is about two feet deep under that. This is a fact about the mud.

I am on camp guard today and how I wish that the good Angel would come with the good tidings of great joy, and that is peace. Soft peace, not piece of bread, for we have had plenty of that ever since we left Madison, but peace, harmony, tranquillity, and the marriage of the opposite parties, that would be glad tidings of great joy in reality.

There has about half of our regt. gone off on a fifteen day scout. They have been gone seven days and we have got marching orders for Mobile and will have to leave before they get back, and that will look wild and my heart flutters as bad as a stage dancer's foot when he is cutting pigeon wings.

Our orders may [be] countermanded, and I hope they will for it is very bad moving now, the mud is so deep. But if they say Go, we will have to trot just like a rich man's dog only we can't trot under the bed.

Jan. 20th. Well, our orders this morning are to be ready
to march for the Riogrand, away down in Mexico. We have
all given up all hopes of our getting back to Wisconsin
again. Oh, when I set out to go to war I left this world behind me. We will probably camp somewhere in Texas until
spring, then here goes to see who is bullet proof. We are all
glad that we are going and would feel disappointed if we
did not go, for we are all ready to start.

We start tomorrow if the overruling Providence is willing. I will probably have a chance to see my brother and
Thomas Stewart as well as many others that I shall be
glad to see. They are all down there somewhere.

Oh well, [here] goes for that painful subject again.
Poor me and poor you! What shall we do? Well, I know
what we can do, but I shan't tell you yet. But here I am
pining away something as you are, all because we have
been disappointed in our love affairs, but fate has it so
and we can't help ourselves.

I believe this is all the news that I can think of, only
that I have drawn a new two-story hat today, and am
proud as can be. Imagine myself at home and bowing very
low to get in somebody's door. Oh, here he is—well there,
if that don't beat the lousy grayback rebs—that young man
that ate the filapean[4] with you at the mill, the one that you
asked me what that or who that fool was, that you had
never seen him. Well, of course, you can't remember him
so I will have to tell you who I mean. It is Chauncey

---

[4] Philopena, or filopena, is a social game in which each of two
persons eats one of the two halves of the kernel of a nut. The one
who is last to say "philopena," or some other word agreed upon,
must pay a forfeit. John Brobst mentions the game several times.

Cooke.[5] He just came along with a package of letters that he has been writing, one of them held up so I could see the backing, and can I believe my eyes? Yes, I can. It was Miss Mary E. Englesby, Gilmanton, Buffalo Co., Wis. Have you ever received it? Of course not. Well, I am in an awful hurry. If I was going to get married to some of them girls that I have disappointed tomorrow I could not be in any more of a fluster, for it is "Do this," "Do that." "Get this ready to load on the wagon." "Get forty rounds of cartridges in your box." "Clean up your gun for inspection." And then my new clothes that I have drawn, I must take time to admire them. With my best wishes, I shall have to close.

The Gilmanton boys are all well. Thompson Pratt is in the Pioneer Corps.[6] He is not with the Co. now. Write soon and often. I will write as often as I can.

We will not be where we can send our letters off at all times and you must not think that I deem them not worth answering if you should not get an answer to all of them. My respects to all you see fit to give and to yourself. Excuse poor writing for I have a poor place to write and am in a great hurry. Direct as I last told you. Yours truly, goodbye for the present.

I remain as your faithful friend,

John F. Brobst   M. E. E.

[5] Private Chauncey H. Cooke, Gilmanton, Wisconsin, Company G, 25th Wisconsin Infantry Regiment.

[6] Similar to engineers, mainly engaged in building roads and bridges.

CHAPTER THREE

February 1864–April 1864

"We say it's all for the Union"

After many a wild rumor and false start, the Twenty-fifth Wisconsin finally left their winter quarters at Helena, Arkansas, on the first day of February, 1864. They were not going to Mobile or Mexico, or out east to help the Army of the Potomac. They were to travel by steamer down the Mississippi River to Vicksburg. There they would join General Sherman, who was planning a deep thrust into the state of Mississippi. Their target was to be a little southern town called Meridian, which was an im-

34

portant link in the South's supply line. General Sherman's
intention was to destroy the town's railroad junction, and
to burn or confiscate the supplies and ammunition stored
in Meridian. The success of such an expedition would be
not only an important military victory, but also a severe
blow to the morale of the entire Confederacy.

The Twenty-fifth Wisconsin Volunteers were ready to
move. They had not been told where they were heading,
but it could not have mattered less, for they were tired
of staying in one place. The winter months in Helena had
been long and tedious; even a rough and muddy march
would be a welcome diversion. If they should have to fight
a few battles along the way, at least they would be con-
tributing more to the Union cause than by the mere performance of guard duty.

Private John Brobst was with his company when it left
Helena on February 1, apparently having recovered from
the recurring attacks of malaria which had troubled him
for months. His treatment had been the usual one pre-
scribed by the army doctors, a cure-all combination of
drugs and quinine. It had done the trick, at least for the
time being. Right now nothing serious was bothering John.
At times he did wonder whether he would ever get home
again, but it seemed futile to speculate on that question.

The only news John had heard about Elsie recently had
come from Mary, and somehow Elsie was becoming less
important to him now. He began looking forward to
Mary's letters for the news she wrote of herself, and the
interest she showed in his activities. She sounded more
grown-up than her years indicated. John enjoyed sharing
his experiences with her and was hoping to see her again
if he ever returned to Wisconsin.

John was in good health and high spirits as the spring campaign began. He and the others were anxious to get on with the war, and to end it as soon as possible. In the course of their service with General Sherman, these volunteers would become famous for their bravery and perseverance; but they would acquire a less desirable reputation for their part in the wholesale destruction and pillage which accompanied their marches. When Sherman's troops returned from this Mississippi expedition, they left behind them a pile of rubbish known as Meridian, and a wide path of smoke and ashes across the state of Mississippi. Sherman's goal had been attained, and his foot soldiers had learned how to travel fast and to live off the land. It had been a difficult lesson at times, but it was just a prelude to the real task of marching and fighting which awaited them on the road to Atlanta.

Camp Near Vicksburg
February[1] the 7th /64

Dear Friend Mary,

I have just received your welcome letter and I was more than glad to hear from you and to hear that you are well. I am well and all right yet.

I am writing to you by the light of a camp fire out of doors because I have been so busy ever since we got back that I have not had time to write.

[1] "February 7" here seems an error for "March 7." The letter describes the Meridian Campaign, which took place during the middle and latter part of February.

We only got back yesterday. We have had a long and hard march, since I last wrote you. We have gone through the state of Mississippi. You have undoubtedly heard of General Sherman's[2] great ride. We were in it. We left every town that we passed through in ashes. The first place was Jackson, the next Morton, Brandon, Hillsboro, Meridian, and Marion. That was as far as we went out that way.

At Meridian we captured ten thousand stands of small arms, three trains of cars and burned them all up and destroyed about 50 miles of railroad.[3] We stopped at Marion 4 days, then we started back to another route and came to Canton. There we stopped 3 days. There we captured 28 railroad engines, destroyed them with several miles of the track, and a lot of us boys had some fun on one of the engines. We carried water all day to fill the boiler of one of them to have a ride. We got it all steamed up, blew the whistle and started up the road. After we got tired of that fun we moved the track [from] where it was about 30 feet down onto level ground and let the steam out and let it go and it struck head first and blew up. That was fun for us.

We burned up 11 towns, captured 10,000 mules and horses and the Lord knows how many darkies for I don't, but everything looks black with them. We did not have much fighting to do, for the rebs ran so that we could not catch them. The woods were full of trunks and boxes filled up with dresses, bed clothes, and all manner of stuff that they thought they had hid from us, but hide from a Yankee soldier if you can. We had some very hard times

[2] General William Tecumseh Sherman.
[3] See Roesch, "Memorandum," p. 9, describing this operation.

and some very good times. As long as there was plenty to eat in the country, we had plenty, and when that ran out our rations ran out and we had to live on parched corn for twelve days. Then was the hard times. March twenty miles a day and nothing but parched corn to eat, then you can hear the boys say, "Oh, if I was home I never would enlist again." But now we have plenty again and feel all right, but we are preparing for another tramp. The orders came today to fit out in new clothes and be ready to march in two days. Where we are going I cannot tell. Up the river I think.

Well, I wish old Jeff and all his gang were in the regions of the low lands where sinners go, and I was Commander in Chief. I would take them through a course of tactics that has not been heard of in modern times.

We were 25 thousand strong on this raid and the rebs say 42 [thousand]. Now you can see by that how near they came to it. They acknowledged they had 23 thousand but did not have enough to risk a battle with us. Oh, the poor Godforsaken cowards. I am ashamed of them, if they are not ashamed of themselves.

I wish this war would end and let us go home, but I don't believe it will end in two years yet. Well, I have got my time more than half out now and the last half goes faster than the first half. At least, it seems so.

The Army of the Potomac has never done anything and never will. If they had done half as much as the western army, this war would have been rubbed out before this time. This army will have to go down there and take Richmond for them, poor fellows.

My learning to sing and play on the violin has played

out, for just as I got the note books, we had to start. All I learned was a few letters of the notes.

Well, Mary, I do wish you would get your picture taken and send it to me. I should be more than glad to get it. Please send it as soon as you can. If you do not believe that my youngest sister does not look like you, when you are over to Mr. Allen's,[4] just have Mrs. Allen show you the picture that I sent home that has two ladies in one frame —they are both my sisters—and see for yourself.

Thomas Stewart[5] enlisted for three years unless sooner discharged. The same way with myself, and I think I shall have to stay the three years out and so will all the boys that went when I did, for this war is a long way from being played out yet.

We have got a lot of new recruits. They are green as we were when we first came out. They make real nice playthings for us. We have our own fun with them, and call them four hundred dollar men. They do not like it very well, but it can't be helped. We do not want them. We wanted to be consolidated with an old regiment and let the new recruits go in a regiment by themselves.

I heard that you had grown so that I would not know you[6] if I was to see you. Now, Mary, I tell you what, if you grow out of my remembrance, I shall have to punish you severely when I get back.

I wish I could have been up there to go to the dance

---

[4] The Allens were John's foster parents.

[5] Thomas Stewart was a friend of John's in another regiment.

[6] One of the recruits from home must have passed along some favorable information about Mary. John's interest in her noticeably changes at this point.

the 22nd, but we were tramping along two hundred miles back in this state playing all kinds of tunes, colors flying, for it was Washington's birthday and we let the rebs know that his old flag should fly yet.

Well, Mary, you will not believe that Elsie has soured on me. Now I am sorry, for you know what becomes of the unbeliever. I would exhort you to repentance if I was up there so that I could, but for me to write it, why it would all get cold before it reached you. Now, Mary, if you believe it or not, it is true.

It is very warm here. Peach trees are all out in bloom. In thirty days we marched four hundred miles. You must not think strange if your letters are not all answered promptly, for I will answer them as soon as I get them. We will have to be marching around so that I can't get them, but I hope you will write often. I shall answer them all as fast as I get them. I love to get letters from friends when I come in after such a march.

I shall have to close for the present. Direct as usual, write soon. My respects to all. Good-by. Yours truly, a true friend,

John F. Brobst

P.S. Excuse poor penmanship for I have a very poor chance to write.

Cairo, Ill., March the 27th. /64

Dear Friend Mary,

It was with much pleasure that I received your ever-welcome letter. Was glad to hear from you and to hear that you are all in good health. My health is very good.

Well, now for the news, and I have not much to write, only that we have got back north as far as Cairo. From here we will go to Virginia, I expect. At least that is the general opinion, and I expect we will have to go and take Richmond for the Army of the Potomac and if they send us there we will take it or we will all die in the attempt. We always take every place that we attempt to take down here, and if our Grant goes with us down there, we will take Richmond for them, and get them started and see if they will help themselves then.

We are most all of us like chickens in the fall of the year. It is so much colder here than it was down where we were. We are getting so that we love the famed land of Dixie.

On the way up here the boat landed at Helena and I jumped off. The boat went off and left me, and you would have laughed to see me dodge around to keep the provost guard from taking me for a deserter. But I landed here safe three days after the regiment got here.

Well, here it is. I have got to go and drill those new recruits. Give us plenty to do, we have to drill in order to teach them. It makes it much harder for us, as we are well drilled and now we have to drill as much as they do. The colonel says they will learn so much faster.

I am afraid I can't write you a very long letter this time, for we have not had any chance—only coming up the river —and could not see much that was new, but I will think of everything that I can and perhaps we will have a good lengthy letter yet. One that will answer, at least.

Well, in the first place, we will not stay here more than a day or two. The colonel came around since I commenced this letter. He says we are going to have a harder march this time than we ever have had yet, and says we had better send everything home that we don't need with us.

If they are going to put us through harder than they did the last march, I pity all the boys as well as myself. We had to march from twenty to twenty-five miles per day, and live on parched corn at that, but we say it's all for the Union. We are not sick of the cause yet, and never will be as long as there is one rebel left to raise his hand to oppose us. Every time that we have a hard time, we like it better and love the Union the more.

Why, I tell you if they had come around with the papers we would all [have] re-enlisted after we had lived on parched corn one week. We had to live [on it] for two weeks [once].

General Sherman gave one brigade a chance to re-enlist, and all that there was left of the four regts. was 130 men. This was doing well, living on parched corn at the time and did not know how long we would have to live on it, and did not care as long as it was hurting the rebs more than it was us. We have not been in the service long enough to re-enlist yet. They have to be in two years, but we have been in only about 20 months yet.

I think I shall wait until my time is out before I go in for three years more, for fear the rebs get my scalp, and then I should be in a fine fix—three years to serve after I am dead.

If your father enlists in the infantry, this is the best regiment in the south. We call ourselves so and the general came and told us himself that we were the best regt. he had on the raid.

Sixteen months more and we expect to see sweet home,

if the rebs don't object to our going north and give us a land warrant for a farm down here about six feet long and three feet wide. There [are] lots of such warrants.

We expect the rebs will run as fast as we can and the consequences will be that we will have to run after them. We will go through Alabama and Georgia and Tennessee to get to Richmond. It is a long route and we will have to suffer a great sight before we get through, but we are all anxious for the word "March."

Well, here I am on another sheet of paper and you did not ask Elsie if she did not wish I was there. I am glad that you did not, for fear she would have said No. Then I should have felt worse than ever. But if you say that you want me to take revenge on little Dan for your and my wrongs, of course I shall have to do it. Oh, if I get at him he will think old Jeff has spoken for him.

We had a windup party last night here. All the secesh gals in town was here to it. We had a good time of it. We danced all night till broad daylight but left something undone, for we did not go home with the girls in the morning. And if we had been up north we surely would not have left that part undone, for that is the best part of all, for then we can put in the variations as we did going up to Dan's last winter. You remember no doubt.

Well, this is about all that I can think of, only I shall express that present home and you must call to Mr. Allen's and get it. If you do not like to ask for it, they will give it to you without. It is a splendid gilt book. I lent it to some of the boys and got it soiled some, but I think it is real nice yet. Give my respects to your folks and to all who you see fit so to do. Well, shall have to close as my paper is almost out, and I am most frozen out and nearly played

out and I expect I shall soon be rubbed out and I scarcely
know what I am about. I shall close hoping an early answer. Direct John F. Brobst, Co. G, 25th Wis., via Cairo,
Ill. Yours truly. As ever. Good-by for the present.

A friend

JFB
MEE

Do not forget to write me about that picture of yours.

[Alabama
April, 1864]

[*Beginning of letter missing and one repetitive passage
about Elsie omitted.*]

Well now, I deny of ever being engaged to her[7] in the
world or ever thinking of it. I went with her for a few
times, but I am not so love cracked as to engage myself to
one like her. I consider myself a better judge of human nature than all that. They might as well say I was engaged to
Queen Victoria and come as near to the truth as when
they say I was engaged to her. That ring, I have got the
way that she came by that, was by putting it on her finger
and I had not the face to ask her for it. But after all that,
she has soured on me, hard luck for me. My heart is
broken. Now this is just as the thing is. Keep this all to
yourself, and in me you will always find a friend.

You are right when you say that I know where Camp
Randall is, and I never want to see it while I am a soldier.
I got enough of that place long ago. I had rather be down

[7] Mary's Aunt Elsie.

here marching twenty miles a day and living on parched corn. I would like to get back to Wisconsin well enough, but deliver me from Camp Randall. We all dread that place worse than we do old Jeff Davis' pills that his men send at us. I expect I never will be there again while I am a soldier.

Tell me what Elsie told you. I will never tell. I just want to know for the fun of it. You say you don't know as I would like it. Well, it must be very bad if I should not like it. I have written her some mighty soft letters as well as her own. Mine were lovesick ones and hers were love-sicker ones.

I wish I had been up there to that dance too. I bet you did not have a better time than we did going up to Dan Hadley's the morning after the dance up to the mill. You did not have that strong arm of protection of Dan's around you. Of course not, but if I had been there I should have stormed the castle, or had some breakfast that is sure, for you see I am a soldier and brave as a sheep.

And then I am glad I was not there for Elsie being there. She would have bestowed her smiles and charms on some other, and that would have killed me dead as a door nail, so you see everything works for the best. Fate is on my side part of the time, don't you think so? I know you do.

I am glad that you have got that book. I am sorry that I got it soiled so bad before I sent it to you. You say you wish you had something to send me in return, but never mind about that. You got that filapean on me so nice that it was worth five times as good a present as that, but when I get back I will pay you for that. You must not forget that we have another on first sight of you. I will surely beat you on that one and that will be worth something.

We had some fun chasing old General Forrest,[8] a rebel; you have heard of his taking Union City and Paducah, Ky. We followed him for seven days but could not catch him. He got one of our company prisoner but for fear we would get him back with the others that he had, he paroled them, and they have gone home to stay until they are exchanged, and that will be some time as they don't exchange prisoners at present. They are lucky for once, but they may thank us that they are not in Libby prison. They took nine of our regt. prisoners.

You will hear of brisk times down here soon, for General Grant is closing in on them all the time. Every day or two we send out a division and drive them back a little ways. They must soon fight or leave Alabama entirely. If they stop and fight they will have to leave, and if they don't fight they will have to leave, so I think the best thing for them is to go without fighting. It would suit me the best anyway, for they shoot careless as can be. They had just as leave hit and kill us as not. It is all wrong, decidedly wrong, but they say that a continual dropping of water will wear away a rock, and if this is true, we will soon have them all worn out, for they are wearing away all the time. Every man and woman down here is loyal as soon as a soldier comes around the house. They will say, "I am Union and always have been. You will not take my chickens and turkeys, will you?" But we have no respect of persons down here. They must all suffer alike.

The people up north do not know what war is. If they were to come down here once, they would soon find out

[8] General Nathan B. Forrest. See account of this engagement in Grant, *Personal Memoirs*, II, 137–38.

the horror of war. Wherever the army goes, they leave nothing behind them, take all the horses, all the cattle, hogs, sheep, chickens, corn and in fact, everything, and the longer the rebs hold out the worse it is for them.

If Elsie has her hair shingled, she must look like a banty hen or a Shanghai rooster.

Well, I must close for the present and I guess you will be glad that I did by the time that you get this all read. Please keep that part of the letter a secret that I have told you to keep. The boys from Gilmanton are all well. Write soon and often and I will do the same, for I like to hear from you often. Excuse poor penmanship. Direct to the Co. and Regt. via Nashville, Tenn.

Nothing more at present, but my respects to all who you see fit to give.

Yours truly, a faithful friend,

John F. Brobst to M. E. Englesby

CHAPTER FOUR

May 1864–August 1864

"Atlanta will soon be ours"

In April of 1864 General Sherman massed his troops at Chattanooga and prepared for a showdown with Johnston's Confederate army which stood between him and Atlanta. Sherman's objective was twofold: he was to destroy Johnston's army, and capture Atlanta, which would then be stripped of its economic potential.[1] By the first week in May, Sherman's army of over ninety thousand

[1] See Sherman's account of the Atlanta campaign, Commager (ed.), *The Blue and the Gray*, II, 929–33.

men outnumbered the Southerners nearly two to one, and the hundred-mile march southeast to Atlanta was begun. The rebel army was firmly entrenched in the hills, and would not give up any strategic position without first taking a high toll in Union casualties. Although Johnston's troops would be forced steadily backward during the following two months, they would manage to avoid an all-out battle with the overwhelming Union army. Sherman would be forced to outmaneuver Johnston as well as outnumber him, and he had just the right kind of men to do the job.

Among Sherman's troops was the Army of the Tennessee under General James B. McPherson, making up about one-fourth of Sherman's army. The Twenty-fifth Wisconsin Regiment was a part of this singular force which was called everything from "an armed mob" to "the best army in the world." These western volunteers still had not absorbed much in the way of army discipline or respect for rank, but they made up for it with their courage and high morale. And they had learned a few special skills which General Sherman could now put to good use. The Twenty-fifth Wisconsin, and the entire Army of the Tennessee, knew how to march and how to dig. During the spring and summer months of 1864 they would do little else, while being under fire almost constantly. While they marched, they carried their spades along with them, and when they could no longer move they dug in and built breastworks and settled down to trench warfare. This was the new way of fighting, and it seemed less dramatic than head-on battles. But trench warfare actually resulted in a high rate of casualties, as the armies were in some degree of contact every day.

General Sherman used the veterans in the Army of the Tennessee for wide flanking movements in an attempt to surround Johnston's troops. These Union soldiers could move fast, and marched almost constantly for over a month, keeping the Confederate army occupied with protecting its rear while the remainder of Sherman's troops continued to push on toward Atlanta.

As the Confederate troops retreated, they tore up bridges and railroad tracks behind them and left nothing that could be of any use to Sherman. In addition to the rebuilding jobs to be done, Sherman's men had to march in strange country, over hills and through woods, streams, and mud. Fatigue, blisters, and sunstroke were common complaints, and food supplies began to dwindle. As the supply line from Chattanooga grew longer, the rations of hardtack, "sowbelly," and coffee became skimpier, and there was no opportunity to supplement the poor diet by foraging in the countryside. While marching, they could seldom take time even to make coffee or cook their meat. The men slept in the open, a few hours at a time, and went for weeks without washing or changing clothes. This campaign was a true test of their quality, and these veterans rose to the challenge. Their spirits never faltered, and they were proud of the hardships they had endured. The march to Atlanta was to be their greatest ordeal and finest performance.

By August, the Confederate troops had retreated to trenches around Atlanta; Sherman's men dug in and waited for the city's surrender. It would be a costly victory for the Union and for General Sherman, who had lost thousands of his best men, among them his priceless General McPherson.

The soldiers themselves were to pay the highest price of all, some with their lives or those of their best friends, and others with an arm or leg. A general breakdown in the health of the troops would soon be evident, as another rash of malaria and dysentery broke out. Of all the Gilmanton boys in the Twenty-fifth Wisconsin Infantry Regiment, John Brobst was for a while the only one not actually disabled by a wound or disease. One of his friends would lose his life in battle. The others, ill and weary, would spend months recuperating at home or in hospitals. Before long, John would join them on the sick list as his health also began to fail.

[Kingston, Ga.]

[Beginning of letter missing.]
Well, here comes a train of cars in now. Just think of it, six days ago the rebs held this railroad for one hundred miles north of this place, and as they retreated they destroyed the track, burned down the bridges, and in six days the bridges were all rebuilt, the track laid and the cars running as far as Kingston and Rome in the very heart of the Southern Confederacy, and they can't help themselves no more than so many babes. It is rather a poor institution I think that cannot support themselves.

I think if kind fortune smiles on us for the next six months as it has for the last one month all of us that are alive will have the unspeakable pleasure of seeing our good homes and have the great pleasure of saying peace has been declared and we be proud of our triumph.

Now, Mary, I have always said I never would discour-

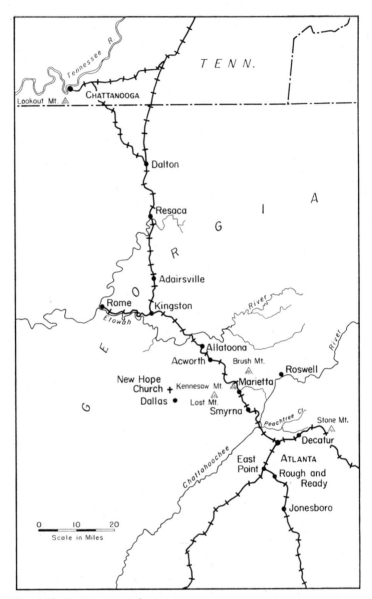

From Chattanooga to Atlanta

age any person in regard to enlisting, but if I was in your father's place I should not enlist, for he has a family and there is enough that has none, that can go better than he can. If I had a family I should never [have] enlisted. There are plenty of ways to get clear of a draft, and make money while he is doing it. Go and hire out for a government teamster or a brakesman on the cars, get thirty-five or forty dollars per month while they are drafting, then quit and go home about your business and it [is] nobody's business. I should not try to stop or say one word to keep any other man from enlisting. It is very hard to be a soldier. No matter how bad the weather is you must go. If it rains you must stand or sleep out, with not as much as a leaf to shelter you from the storm. Perhaps have about half a meal for two days, and that the poorest kind of living. Well, the amount of it—Gilkey's[2] table is a king's table beside what we have in the army. This is not the case at all times, for when we are where we can get it we have plenty, and that which is good, but the most of the time we are on the move and then we cannot get such as is fit for a man to eat.

Now, I will tell you as near as I can what the load is that a soldier has to carry, and march from 15 to 25 miles a day. He has a gun that weighs 11 pounds, cartridges and cartridge box about 6 pounds, woolen blanket 3 pounds, rubber blanket 5 pounds, two shirts, two pairs of drawers about 3 pounds, canteen full of water which they oblige you to keep full all the time, which is about 6 pounds, then three or five days' rations, which will weigh about 8 pounds, and then your little trinkets that we need, perhaps

[2] The Gilkey family of Gilmanton, Wisconsin.

2 pounds, makes a total of about 45 or 50 pounds. That is what makes us think of our homes in these hot days.

Well, I must tell you what I have been doing today. I have been washing all the forepart of the day. You would have thought I was some old maid washing away there all alone, no one to bother me at all. I can wash, cook, sew, do anything as well as any of the girls. I will be all ready to keep a bachelor's hall when I get home. Then my sign over the door will be, "Positively no admittance for ladies."

I wish the people up north would send them tormented old baches off to the war up there, or they will steal all the girls away from us by the time that we get back, and we will have to wait for the young ones to grow up. Oh, if I really knew that this would be the case I should try and get shot, I do believe. What a good thing it is that we cannot read the future, do you not think so?

Well, I must stop and go and see if I can't find a secesh sheep that is playing the spy on us, and will have to be shot and have his bones picked. Oh, I am one of the lowest grade of men. I go right in a man's yard, steal a sheep, hog or chicken, cow or anything that I can find, take off a corpse before the eyes of the owner, and if [he] says anything tell him to dry up or he will get his wind shut off for a year or two. I expect all such kinds of animals will run and yell as soon as they see us coming home. [*Rest of letter missing.*]

I would send you a stamp, but I haven't got another one **with me.**

Camped in the field in Georgia
May the 20th /64

Dear Friend Mary,

It was with the greatest of pleasure that I received your ever-welcome letters. I was very glad to hear from you and to hear that you are well. I am well at present. Hope this will find you still enjoying the same blessing.

I do not know when you will get this, for we are where it is a hard matter to send a letter off and I hope you will not think strange of me for not answering your letters. I have written to you every time that I could send it off. I have received two from you and will answer them both in this one.

We have had very stirring times down here. We have had plenty of hard fighting for the last two weeks. Our regiment was under fire for three days and nights without being relieved, and during that time we only lost twenty-six men.

We charged on some rifle pits that another regiment charged three times but could not take them. General Dodge[3] sent us to try it, and we took them and held them, killing and wounding a great many of the enemy, some of which fell in our hands. None of the Gilmanton boys were hurt. Luck was on our side for once, at least. We gained a complete victory, routed the rebs after about four days fighting, and are at the present time in hot pursuit. We have driven them about 60 miles. The large fight came off

[3] General Grenville M. Dodge, commanding 16th Army Corps, of which the 25th Wisconsin was a part. The action described took place near Resaca, Georgia.

at Dalton and thereabouts. We captured two trains of cars here last night and one ton of gun powder, forty wagons, and 2,300 prisoners. I wish I had time to tell you all about it from the commencement, but I have not, so I shall have to wait and tell you some other time. We are getting close on to Atlanta now. There we expect one of the hardest battles of the war. Then I hope we can have a little rest. We rested all last night, the first night that we have rested all night since we left Decatur, Ala. Night before last, we marched all night, only stopped long enough to make up a little coffee. We are almost tired out. We are all ready to go to the last; we want to wind the thing up and get home if we live to ever go back. The rebs have almost 80 thousand men and we have about 125 thousand men, but they have forts and rifle pits while we have to take the field. I do not know when you will get this, but I shall write a little every day until I get a chance to send it off. I do not know when that will be, but I shall have it ready to send the first opportunity.

It is a splendid country here and I do not see how the rebs can fight much longer for a cause that is as hopeless as the one that they are fighting to establish. The longer they keep up the war, the worse they are off. When I get back, I can tell you all about it, for I can talk better than I can write and had rather talk with you than to write.

That Fort Pillow[4] massacre was a horrible thing, but our soldiers make them pay for it down here. There was one of the Iowa regiments charged on a rifle pit, and

[4] Fort Pillow was a Union garrison near Columbus, Kentucky, comprising over 500 troops, of which about half were colored. On April 12, 1864, the garrison was attacked and virtually destroyed

twenty-three of the rebs surrendered but the boys asked them if they remembered Fort Pillow and killed all of them. When there is no officer with us, we take no prisoners. We want revenge and we are bound to have it one way or the other. They must pay for those deeds of cruelty. We want revenge for our brother soldiers and will have it.

You must not think for one moment that I blame you for writing what you did to me, for I think that you did perfectly right, but really Mrs. Allen is laboring under a mistake, but then she is not to blame for what she hears but I know she never heard me say that I was engaged to anyone, but she is the best of women. She has been a perfect mother to me, and I shall always remember her for it.

But now let them work away, let them all say that I have been engaged and I shall say that I am not and we will see who will gain the day, but I think that I shall win myself. Man knoweth not at what hour the Son of Man cometh and if I ever live to get back perhaps you will know where my cherished hopes are, and perhaps it will be one that you least expect.

Well, I hope Elsie did find out something that will do her good. I am of your opinion about having that other Mary in preference to Elsie, but then Elsie is a good girl for all that I know, but after all as you say but then there is something lacking and that something is energy and

---

by a rebel force under General Forrest. What incensed the Northerners were reports that the Union troops, especially the colored soldiers and their families, had been indiscriminately slaughtered after their capture. See a contemporary account in Pratt, *Civil War in Pictures*, pp. 196, 199.

neatness, and that is a great item, but she is not to blame
for it, for it is the way that she has been raised. The man
that she said saw my picture was John W. McKay[5] when
he was home on a furlough last fall, but she said it was
in that way that he happened to see it and it was the
case. And you say that it is not so, and I believe you, but
even if it was so, it would not kill anyone, and I shall live
through the shock I think, but it is almost as severe as the
shock of a galvanic battery, for she has soured on me.

Well, Mary, little Dan is here all right, running around
feeling as proud as a pea fowl, for you see he got a letter
from Mary Ames the other day, and it had two or three
pipes of smoking tobacco in it, and I should judge from
that they have formed a treaty of peace, something like
the Indians. They have smoked the pipe of peace and oh,
then she called him her Dan. Wasn't that real nice! How
sweet, honey is nowhere compared with it.

Thompson Pratt is in the Pioneer Corps and while he
was rolling a large log out of the road, he heard a noise
that arrested his attention, and going around to the end
of the log, he found that it was hollow. Then he peeked
in and saw something and made a grab and caught it.
"And," Thompson says, "by Christ, it was a rebel officer."
And on looking around they found another in the same
log. They had hid in the log but got caught at their own
game.

We have some fun as well as hard times. Then I have
captured one prisoner myself but I shot him through the
leg before I took him. You see I did not want to play a
game with him that two could play at, for he might beat

[5] Lt. John W. McKay, Gilmanton, Wisconsin, Company G, 25th
Wisconsin Infantry Regiment.

me out, and the prisoner be on the other side of the question. Better sure than doubtful in times of war.

Well, I shall have to close for the present, but perhaps I will have a chance to write some more before I have the chance to send this off. If I do have time to write more I will do so.

Good for me. The best luck in the world is in store. The mail goes out today, the same day that I commenced this, so I hope you will soon receive this.

We have got the news here that General Lee has got defeated in Virginia and is marching for this place to try and check us. If they do not check us, we will go right down to the Gulf. We are repairing the railroad as fast as we go, so that the cars can soon run in here where we are. If we gain the day here, the rebellion will soon close, in my opinion. God speed the day, for I am tired of war.

Pratt has just come down to the regt. He says he never found any reb officers in a log, so the man that told it made a mistake.

Well, Mary, I shall have to close for the present, hoping you will have good times and enjoy yourself well, and write often to one that has the air for a house, the heavens for a shelter in stormy days and nights. Excuse poor writing, for it is very poor. Write often, direct as your last. I remain yours as ever, yours truly, good-by,

John F. Brobst

[*Beginning of letter missing.*]

Sunday Morning the 22nd. Tomorrow morning we start on our long tramp and if I have any chance to write while

on the march, I will do so. If not, you know the reason.
Our col. told us last night that we were going to have a
hard time and if the enemy did not run, we would [have]
to do some hard fighting, and tear up railroad track.

This morning, there were five companies of rebs came
in and gave themselves up, with nine officers. There were
one hundred and seventy-three men in the five companies.
This is the largest squad that I have ever seen come in at
any one time. They say they are sick of the war and want
peace on any terms. That is what we want, but we want
it on our terms, not any, but one only, and that is nothing
more than an unconditional surrender of themselves and
all that belongs to them. Those are our terms and that is
what we will have or fight them for the next ten years.
Myself as well as all of the other soldiers have got so that
we hate and loathe the sight of any of the poor miserable
half-starved brutes, but the men are not to blame as much
as their officers. That Fort Pillow as well as Lawrence[6]
massacre is what we can't swallow very well. We always
have to throw it up to every reb that we see.

There was a train of cars went out a few moments ago
with, I should judge, about two thousand prisoners that
we took yesterday. They look very hard. They say they
have not half enough to eat when they are in camp and
much less when they are on the march. Our men would
not stay here one month if they had to live as the rebs
have to live.

Those deserters that came in this morning tell a good

[6] Lawrence, Kansas, a strongly abolitionist town which was attacked and nearly destroyed by Confederate guerrillas on August
20, 1863. See Pratt, *Civil War in Pictures*, pp. 133–34, for a contemporary account.

story for us if it is true, but I do not put much dependence in what they say. You see, this place where we now are is where the reb Johnston intended to make a stand, but did not do it, and those deserters say that he called up his men and asked them if they were going to fight or not, that if they did not fight better at Atlanta than they did at Dalton he would hoist the stars and stripes and surrender the entire command. The prisoners say all was still as death itself, not a murmur against the stars and stripes was spoken. One feared the other. I have no doubt that if every man that was there had known the feelings of the others that they would have given three cheers for the brave old flag and said, "Raise the noble emblem," but one dared not tell his mind for fear the next one would run him through with his bayonet.

Well, Mary, I am going to tell you something that you will hardly believe. When we were out so long on the battlefield that I spoke of in my last, we had to have a little sleep, so one part of the regiment would lay down among the flying balls and the roar of cannon and muskets and go to sleep, and sleep as sound as though he was at his quiet home. It sounds nice to hear the rattle of the cannon and muskets and shell, grape, and cannister balls and everything making its peculiar noise. It certainly is music. It is not in times of action that chills the blood, but after the action when you see your comrades with arms and legs shot off and mangled in all forms. Those are the hardest sights of the battlefield. The battle that I have mentioned is our first real experience.

General Woods[7] has issued an order to compliment our

[7] Brigadier General Charles R. Woods, commanding Third Brigade, First Division, 15th Army Corps, Army of the Tennessee.

regt. for its good conduct on the battlefield. It was a good one. Perhaps you will see it in some of the papers soon. We saved his brigade from being captured and he renders us his sincere thanks for the timely rescue.[8] He is a very able general and knows how to appreciate a good act. The order was read to us last evening. It is a good one.

Well, now for the little fixings and a halt. Thompson Pratt has just come down to the Co. on a visit. He wanted to know where I was writing to. I told him to Gilmanton. He says tell them he is well and got the ague in the bargain. Dan is here all right and has got him a new pair of shoes, not boots any more. Boots have played out. Boots cost from ten to fifteen dollars here and Dan can't go that. His colts is too small to stand that. Dan and Hank Morse[9] and Chauncey Cook all tent together, all of them old maids, and they are the most interesting set you ever saw. One is so afraid that he will do a little more than the other that none of them will do anything, so they get no vittles half of the time.

I have tented with O. N. Hilliard[10] of Mondovi for the last eight months. The old maids were too much for me. I could not go them so I left their bed and board.

Well, this is Sunday but I guess I will not go to Sunday School today for I am afraid the young ladies will be look-

[8] Probably referring to the support given to Woods' brigade in the capture of an important hill near Resaca which had been held by Confederate troops under General Polk. See Johnson and Buell (eds.), *Battles and Leaders of the Civil War*, IV, 282.

[9] Private Henry L. Morse, Mondovi, Wisconsin, Company G, 25th Wisconsin Infantry Regiment. He died of disease April 6, 1865, at Goldsboro, North Carolina.

[10] Corporal Obed N. Hilliard, Mondovi, Wisconsin, Company G, 25th Wisconsin Infantry Regiment.

ing at me, and I will have no such work for it grieves me because Elsie would not like to have them look at me. Is not that a good reason?

I wish I was up to Gilmanton. How I would storm around and make the people think that a regular jimmy cane was coming, but I am not there and I guess I will not go up today, for I could not get there until after noon and then I would not have much time to stay, so I will not go today.

We had good news from the Army of the Potomac, if it is all true. You have heard the same I suppose, as all the news that we get from there comes by the way of papers from the north. If half of what we hear is true, the war cannot last many months longer, and I hope it is better than we have heard.

Oh, I will be so glad if I ever do get back that I will not know what to do with myself, for I am tired of being bound down in one place all the time. If I want to go outside of the camp I must ask just like a small schoolboy, and if they say that I can go, why I go, and if they say I cannot, I must stay.

I shall be glad when I can go and come when I have a mind to, and come when I please, and no one's business. But I have stood it for nearly two years and I guess I can stand it for one more year and then good-by to all masters, for I shall be my own man once more.

Dan is writing to dear Mary Ames. He is cross as a bear with a sore head. He does not want anyone to speak to him while he is writing. It must be real nice. He did not get any letters from her for a long time, but the other day he got one with some tobacco in it. They have made peace I guess. That looks like it at least, do you not think so?

Well, I guess I have written all the nonsense and news that I can think of at this time.

You say you have not fault to find about my using you well. I hope you will not ever have any fault to find in that respect. I am glad of your friendship and hope mine will be received as readily as that of yourself. I ask and request your friendship and confidence. You already have mine. I would trust you farther than any person living. You may not believe this but it is true as I live, and I really hope that the confidence that I place in you will never be deceived. What confidence you place in me shall never be deceived.

I will close for the present. Hope to hear from you soon. Direct as last I told you. My respects to your folks as well as yourself. Good-by.

> From a faithful
> Friend, John F. Brobst
> to Mary E. Englesby

Our Travels from the 23rd of May

Orders to march at 8 o'clock in the morning, but did not get started until twelve on the night of the 23rd. Marched all that night until noon the next day, and then rested four hours by the side of the splendidest spring that I ever saw. Then took up our march again and marched to a small town called Danforth, arrived at this place about sunset. Here we camped for the night after a march of about thirty miles without any sleep. Then to cap it off it rained all night and we had no tents. The result is, here I sit on the morning of the twenty-fourth rather uncomfortably wet, but the sun shines quite warm; will soon march again. Some excercise with a hot sun will dry us off so we will soon feel better. Boys [are] cursing old Jeff Davis, wanting him tied up to a fence post and let the grasshoppers to kick him to death. Very good way for him to die I think, don't you? We will see what will happen today. We are on our way to Atlanta, Georgia.

May the 25th. We start on the march about ten o'clock, march very slow but march nearly the whole of the night as well as all of the day. Rained very hard the forepart of the night, very disagreeable.

May the 26th. Start early in the morning drawn up in line of battle, slight skirmishing, we take the town of Calis,[11] Georgia, without much opposition. Camped where I now write about three o'clock in the afternoon. Orders came while I was writing this note to march. I put away my materials and fell in, but the order being countermanded I resumed my writing. Some cannonading to our left twenty miles west of the Dalton and Atlanta railroad. This is all the particulars of the present day up to dark. We will see what will transpire between this and daylight tomorrow morning.

May the 27th. This morning a few moments after sunrise we were in line of battle where we now remain. We have

[11] John must mean Dallas, Georgia.

gained about forty rods of ground today about 12 o'clock. Our skirmishers are out now. No fighting, only what the skirmishers and artillery are doing, some few balls come over our heads. One of our men in my Co. wounded in the hand. Three in the regiment are all that I know of being hurt up to twelve today. Dan Hadley is sitting by my side smoking his pipe, taking comfort. Eat, drink, smoke and be merry, for tomorrow you may die. I have had your picture out and looking at it but you look as calm and collected, as though there were no prospects of a battle. The rebels are about fifty rods in front of us. I expect we will soon have to charge the hill and storm the castle for them. We will see what this afternoon will bring forth.

About 2 o'clock our skirmishers gained the top of the bluff but were repulsed with heavy loss in killed and wounded. This is all up to dark.

May the 28th in the morning. Still in line of battle. Occasionally a man wounded or killed. No general engagement yet. On the left about one mile was very heavy firing about twelve o'clock last night. Have not heard the result yet but think we have gained ground from the direction of the firing this morning. Issuing rations this morning, only half rations at that. Hard times in store for us undoubtedly. Made our coffee this morning while the rebs were trying to shoot some of us but they did not succeed. Dan is here by my side smoking again. Comfort, of course. Who would not be a soldier? It is very pleasant this morning. We have a line of cannon just in the rear of us. It was planted in the night last night. Have not fired any of it yet. About two o'clock today the orders came to right face,

counter march by file right, then file right, march, then by
the left flank, march, guide center. Next is halt, and here
we are in the rear of an old fence, about fifteen rods nearer
than what we were to our friends that fire their salutes at
us when we approach them. Just went along by here after
a wounded man. Do not know how bad he is hurt. We
dare not show our heads unless we want them to send
one of their whistling jimmies at us. They are not healthy,
so we lay low for young rebs in place of young ducks.
Still cannonading some and skirmishing some.

Some more on the 28th. The rebs made a very desperate charge this afternoon about half past six o'clock.
They came up in a mass three or four columns deep. Our
boys lay concealed behind our breastworks and they came
within 8 rods, then raised and gave them a volley. The
rebs drove us out of two breastworks, captured two pieces
of artillery. (We recaptured the artillery.) Then General
Logan[12] came up with his reserves and drove them back.
It was the orders for our men to fall back and let them
get those pieces of artillery in order for us to get a good
chance to fire on them. Our boys were very willing to be
driven until they drove us far enough. Then came the
destruction of the rebs. Our loss is very light, perhaps two
or three hundred killed and wounded. That of the enemy
is supposed to be two thousand killed and wounded, all
of which now lay on the field between our forces and
their own. We took 150 prisoners with their arms and
accoutrements. After this, night came on. All quiet, except
men working building breastworks. This came off a short

[12] General John A. Logan, commanding 15th Army Corps, Army
of the Tennessee.

distance to the right of us in sight of our regt. but we were not engaged.[13]

Sunday morning, May the 29th. About 7 o'clock. Heavy skirmishing this morning is all that can be heard. We are on a range of mountains I call the Lost Mountains. Prisoners say if they cannot hold those mountains there is no use of their trying to hold Atlanta. Their commander says the same thing. Very pleasant this morning, pleasant all day today. The enemy have been trying to get their dead and wounded all day, but we go into them with vigor and keep them back. I do not think they have succeeded in getting one of them off. We have got ours all taken care of, and a good share of the enemy's taken care of. It is considered a great victory when the dead and wounded fall in the hands of the enemy. This is the reason why we fight so vigorously to hold them.

They lost them in the charge above mentioned. The rebels made seven desperate charges between 12 o'clock on the night of the 27th and 12 o'clock on the night of the 28th. Their loss is estimated at seven thousand in the seven charges, ours five hundred. This is good for us but death on the rebs. General Hardee[14] led the charge here in person. He is the rebel commander. Rumor says that General Hooker[15] has taken 7,000 prisoners today but the news is not reliable yet. Hope it is true. Still heavy skirmishing, balls flying over our heads all the time. We expect a charge on us this evening. If they come we will treat them

[13] Battle of New Hope Church, a few miles north of Dallas.

[14] General William J. Hardee.

[15] General Joseph Hooker, commanding 20th Army Corps, Army of the Tennessee.

to the best we have in our line of business so they should not complain. This is all up to the present time.

May the 30th. Still in front of Dallas in line of battle. Our company out skirmishing, came out this morning. Last night about 12 o'clock, the enemy made a charge on our left and were repulsed. When they came down to our part of the line here they made four as gallant charges as any living soldiers could make. They massed their forces and on they came to have death and destruction dealt out to them. They were allowed to come to within about thirty yards of us before we got the command to fire. We raised up from behind our breastworks and gave them a volley which checked them for a moment, but they soon rallied and on they came, but with the same success as at first. In this charge they rallied three times but then were forced to fall back, but soon they came again and met the same fate. Again they came and again were repulsed and came again the fourth and last time for that night. Braver men never shouldered a musket than those rebels that came up to drive us out of our works. We piled up their dead and wounded in perfect masses. It is horrible. Just think for yourself, thirty cannon throwing grape shot at the rate of twenty pounds every three seconds to each cannon, with ten thousand rifles pouring in the ranks of men.[16]

Our losses are small from the fact that we were in good breastworks while the enemy was advancing on an open field. They had to advance as we have to most of the time. I do not think they lost less than three or four thousand

[16] See Chauncey Cooke's account of this battle in *Wisconsin Magazine of History*, V, 75–80. John brought home a walking stick cut from the battlefield in Pine Woods. It is now a family keepsake.

killed, wounded and prisoners. Our regiment lost only one killed, and four wounded, but some of the other regts. lost more than what we ˙did.

The rebs use no cannons, do not know why. Perhaps they have but little artillery and have taken that in their forts. Atlanta and Richmond ends the war. The Gilmanton boys are all well yet. [*Rest of letter missing.*]

Camped in the field 27 miles from
Atlanta June the 15th/64

Dear Friend Mary,

It was with much pleasure that I received your ever-welcome letter and was more than glad to hear from you and to hear that you are well. I am quite unwell but there is no stopping here. We must go as long as we can and when we cannot go any further we have to lay down along side of the road and get well, die, or let the rebs take you. Oh, when I am sick how tired I get of this war.

They are fighting very heavy now with artillery on both sides. The rebs are in the mountains. It will take a long time yet before we get into Atlanta. We will have to fight every foot of the way. The batteries are throwing shell and solid shot, cutting down trees and everything that comes in the way of the balls. We are not losing very heavy in men yet but do not know how soon we will. The rebs I can't tell anything about, but think they are losing as heavy as we are.

We are on the railroad. Our supplies come in on one end of the road and that of the rebs on the other end. We can hear both of them whistle. It has been very wet here

John F. Brobst in uniform. From
a daguerreotype in the possession of
Margaret Brobst Roth.

John and Mary Brobst with their two
oldest children, about 1873. From
a daguerreotype in the possession of
Margaret Brobst Roth.

WAR, WAR, WAR!!

There will be a grand rally of men, women, and children, at the Congregational Church, Randolph Centre, on

SATURDAY AUG. 2, 1862,

at 2 o'clock P. M., to see what measures can be taken to secure the immediate enlistment of fifty Volunteers from this Town, as that number is required to fill our quota, and save us from disgrace in this time of national peril. The meeting will be addressed by

Hon. HORACE MAYNARD, M. C.

from Tenn., who chose to have his property confiscated rather than forsake the Union.

Hon. JUSTIN S. MORRILL, M. C.

from this State, and other gentlemen from abroad and at home will be present to make speeches.

All who desire not to see our beloved and once honored AMERICA become the prey of lawless ruffians, and the beautiful ensign of our nations liberty trampled under the feet of traitors are invited to be present.

In behalf of the nations cause.

R. HOLDEN, JOHN ROWELL, J. K. PARISH,
JOHN BUSWELL, E. WESTON, J. C. FARGO,
JOHN WESTON, S. A. BABBITT, O. D. ALLIS.

Recruiting poster. Courtesy of State Historical Society, Wisconsin.

Camp Randall, Madison, Wisconsin. Courtesy of Library of Congress.

Setting up winter quarters in Union camp. Courtesy
of State Historical Society, Wisconsin.

Siege of Vicksburg. Courtesy of State Historical Society, Wisconsin.

Battle of Resaca, Georgia. From *Southern Battlefields* (Nashville, 1906).

Rebel works in front of Atlanta. Courtesy of Library of Congress.

Scenes from Atlanta. Courtesy of Library of Congress.

Grand Review of Sherman's Army, Washington, D.C., May 24, 1865. Courtesy of Library of Congress.

Camp near
Raleigh N. C.
April 22nd 165

Dear Mary
              I again take the present
opertunety of writing you a few lines to
let you know of my whereabouts and
how I am getting along I am well and
hope when this comes to hand it will
find you enjoying the same blessing
Well Mary. there is plenty of news to write
and all good news and I shall not tempt
to write it for you have undoubtly heard
all before this it will go through the
loyal States like wild fire I think the
long looked and hoped for peace has come
at last we do not or we cannot appreciate
the glorious news Lee has surendered the army
of Northern Virginia Johnston has called
for an armistics with views resulting to a
permenent peace and the reestablishment
of the laws of the union again we all
think and belive that this cruel war
has reached its end at last

Photograph of original letter.

for some two weeks back. We have no tents and have to take it rain or shine.

Well, Mary, I should like to write more but they are fighting all around us so that I expect we will have to take a hand and help play it out. There was a rebel shell just now busted only a few rods from where I now sit. I thank you for the verses. I think they are real nice.

I expect the first thing I know you will be like the old woman's girl, you will be out of this world of trouble.

The Gilmanton boys are all alive yet but some of them not very well, as myself.

I hope you will excuse a short letter this time and I hope I shall have a better chance to write the next time. I think there are some prospects of this war ending this summer. I hope so, for we have fourteen months to serve yet. That is a long time.

Tell your grandmother I send my best respects in return. My respects to all you see fit to give. Write soon, direct as your last. Good-by for the present.

Yours truly from a friend and wellwisher,

> John F. Brobst
> Mary E. Englesby

[Georgia, July, 1864]

[Beginning of letter missing.]

If we live to get home we will have one gay time. At least we will take the girls through a course of military tactics that will make them wish that there would be another war so that they could get aclear of us for awhile again. Well, I expect you will hate us like poison, for we will be so very fierce after being down here shooting men for three years that everybody will fear us, and may the copperheads fear us for we are going to clean them out as soon as we get home.

If I was at home and went to that dance I could not dance, for I have got to be so lazy that I can hardly breathe now and am getting no better very fast. But then I might pluck up courage enough to go and look on for awhile and then go to sleep after supper. Of course, I should not be cheated out of that. No indeed, better not to go at all than to [have] such a mishap as that befall me.

Well, I might tell you a little story about Thompson Pratt. The other day we were working hard building breastworks.[17] We worked all night and got through the next day about three o'clock in the afternoon, so we made a shade with our blankets and lay down to take a sleep and rest for awhile. We had just got to sleep when the rebs began to throw shell into us. We scrambled up as fast as we could but Pratt, and he said it was a God damn mean caper after we had been working so hard and just get to sleep and then have the rebs throw shell into us. Tom stuck to it like a hero for awhile, but it got too hot for him. He had to climb for protection, as well as the balance of us. I tell you Thompson was awful mad. He swore enough to sink the Southern Confederacy. We have lots of fun with him about them shell that love him so well.

Well, Mary, talk of battle, why you have been in three real pitch battles and any quantity of small skirmishes and you look calm and collected as anyone can look, not a bit of fear do you show, but I am the one that carries you in those places of danger. You will be an old soldier

---

[17] See an officer's description of the building of breastworks, or fortifications, Commager (ed.), *The Blue and the Gray*, II, 939–43.

by the time that I get back. It is a good consolation to have a picture to look [at] sometimes when we get lonesome and homesick. When I look at your picture it seems like home away down here in Georgia. It is all bluffs and mountains just like Buffalo Co. is, plenty of water in the valleys.

How does Elsie get along? I have not heard from her since last winter. Do not know whether she is in the land of living or not. Hope she is, although she has broken my heart. Yet I wish her all the happiness in the world, poor me.

They have got to shooting off their big guns again this morning since I commenced this letter, the rebs as well as our own. They are getting in good earnest about it too. I shall have to close for the present now and be on hand for what may happen. I have told you all the news that I can think of.

I have not heard from you since I last wrote you but shall look for an answer soon to this as well as to the others. The cannonading is getting very heavy. My health is very good. My respects to all. Write soon, direct as your last. Goodbye for the present.

Yours truly,
a friend, John F. Brobst
Mary Englesby

Camped in the Field south of
the Chattahoochee River, July the 11th/64

Dear Friend Mary,

I now take the present opportunity of answering your

ever-welcome letters. As I received two, I shall have to
answer two. The rebels evacuated the Kennesaw Mountains, the place where I wrote to you on the morning of
the third of July. We arose early for this was to be a day
of excitement as we were to charge the entire length of
our lines, and the line being 23 miles long you may
imagine the roar of artillery and musketry. Just think for
one moment, over four hundred pieces of cannon with
about one hundred and fifty thousand rifles on our side
and nearly as many more on the side of the enemy. It
would fairly make the earth quake, but I have heard just
such a noise several times since I have been down here
and expect to hear it a number of times more if the rebs
do not rub me out.

But how did we get clear of this charge? Why, it was
the easiest thing in the world, for when we got [up] in
the morning the rebs were gone.

We followed them very close all that day, until we were
brought to a standstill about three o'clock in the afternoon. Here they had strong works, and we went into camp
of [for] the night, built breastworks, and on the fourth,
about 9 o'clock, we were ordered to charge the enemy
works. We did so and drove them out and took their
places in the works. Our regt. was in the third line, so that
we did not lose many of our members. As the first line
took the works we yelled so hard that the rebs were frightened out of their senses. They fired two volleys, then ran
for sweet life. Now we had them on the go again and
followed them up until they came to the river. Here they
made another stand and we, that is our army corps, were
held in reserve to send either way that we were most
needed, and on the 8th of July we were ordered to march
on the left wing to Rossville,[18] which place we captured on

the ninth and destroyed a cloth factory that gave employ-
ment to five hundred hands, so you may judge how much
clothing the rebs had been getting from this place.

On the afternoon of the tenth we came to the river,[19] but
the bridge was burned down and the rebs were on the
other side of the river, and our work was to cross the
river, so the cavalry went up the river several miles and
crossed over and came down on the rebs with a fierce
charge, and at the same time we jumped into the river
and commenced swimming, wading, falling down, rolling,
and yelling like wild men, and the rebs running for life
again, and the result is here we are on the south side of
the river building works to keep the rebs back, and I think
Atlanta will soon be ours. For when part of an army gets
a foothold the remainder will soon get the same, and
when our army gets all on this side of the river, we can
push forward and the rebels will not have any more mountains to help them to defend the city of Atlanta, but the
country will be comparatively level, which will give us a
much better chance than what we have been having. It is
thought that they will not try to hold the city, as we would
destroy it if they did so, and if not we would save the place
for our own use.

We have very good news from General Grant's army. I
hope he will get Richmond soon, for I am satisfied that
we will soon have Atlanta, and then I think the rebs will
begin to talk peace, but they must come to our terms or
have no peace. Some of them say they will fight as long
as there is one of them left. We tell them that is what
we want. We want to kill them all off and cleanse the
country, but they are very few that talk so. Once in a long
time we find one hot-headed one. The most of them say

---

[18] John must mean Roswell.   [19] Chattahoochee River.

that they are tired of war and want peace, even at our terms.

I hope the war will soon close, but it may last three years longer for all that I know, but I hope it will not last three days longer.

It is very warm here. A person can not take any comfort in the shade. It is as warm in the shade as it is up there in the sun. We had several men sun struck on the way here, but I am all right yet and so is Dan. He is off on detail today, so I have not had a chance to ask him if he remembers the turnover, but no doubt he does. I do very well, and remember what Dan was trying to do, but he failed but says he will win yet.

Well, I have written all the news and now for the fancy fixings. Well, in the first place this morning I went to work and washed my clothes, and you may believe they needed it bad enough, as we have to go a long time that we can't get a chance to wash any. I have had to go thirty days without a change of clothes, marching in the dirt and sweating, and you can well imagine how we look in such cases, and then to top off with, perhaps we will have to lay in rifle pits for a week at a time, but, Mary, there are better times coming. If I live to get out of this safe and sound, I certainly will know how to enjoy home and its comforts. I have only thirteen months more to stay. The time is almost two-thirds gone, and when we get on the last year, time will glide off faster apparently than any other part of the time. Well, to proceed with my story, after I had washed my clothes I came up and went to cooking for myself and partner. He is a young man from Mondovi. His name is Hilliard. We have tented together for nearly one year and live as agreeable as any man and woman in Buffalo County. Dan is too much of an old maid for me to tent with. We call him grandmother in the company. Pratt is in the Pioneer Corps, John Christian[20] is too lazy to live, so this man and I went in for three years, or during the war.

Well now, to go on and tell you what we had for dinner. When I got back from the river, Hilliard had been off and got some green apples, and some parsley and pig weed, and we had stewed apples, greens, beans and rice, hard bread and coffee, pork, and some dough goods I call them, for we got some flour and we have been trying to make some pancakes, but they are like whetstones. We can't make them good at all. We tried to make some apple dumplings, but did not get them fit to eat, but I can make tea and coffee and not burn it.

I wish you would write and tell me how to make pies and rice puddings and apple dumplings and pancakes, and make them light. Tell me what to put in them. They are so heavy is all that is the matter with them.

Now, Mary, I do not like to dispute you, but if Elsie did look pretty it is something new to me. Oh, I tell you I will have a long account to settle with you when I get back, and we will have to come to some terms of peace, for I expect we will have a quarrel, of course we will, but the filapean will be on you, sure as I am a soldier boy.

I had not heard that, that Mary was up to Mondovi, but she is getting handy by. Good for her. I will not have far to go, but I do not know who she is. Perhaps it is some old maid.

Well, orders have come to get ready to march at a moment's notice, and the mail is going out in a few

[20] Private John W. Christian, Gilmanton, Wisconsin, Company G, 25th Wisconsin Infantry Regiment. Killed in action July 22, 1864, near Decatur, Georgia.

moments, so in order to have the thing come out even, I shall have to close for the present. Give my respects to all who you choose. Tell Curt[21] he must rattle the jawbone for me, as I have had to eat so much hard tack that my teeth have become so poor that I can't rattle any more. It is all rattle-headed with me in place of rattle-toothed. Oh, what will we do when the country breaks the war up and scatters soldiers all around? Why, we will go home of course.

Do not forget to tell me how to make those articles in the grub line as we call it, and then when I get back you can come and see me when I am batching, and help me eat some of them. I will close for the present, hoping to hear from you soon. Address as your last. Goodbye for the present but I hope for a short time only. Write soon.

From a friend,

John F. Brobst

Tell your father to write.
Mary E. E.

Grand flourishes
on these letters. Oh, how expert
with a pen. Goodbye. Me.

Camped Near Atlanta, Ga.
[August, 1864]

Dear Friend Mary,

It was with much pleasure that I received your ever-welcome letter and was more than glad to hear from you and to hear that you are well and hearty. It found me

[21] Mary's brother.

well and hearty too, and I hope when this comes to hand it will find you enjoying the same blessing.

I thank you for what you told me about baking pancakes, for I have tried some of them and they were light and good, and I will bet if you had been here and right hungry you would have said the same thing.

There is not much news to write at present. Both armies are laying still for the present, watching one another to see how and where the other will jump, just like two great savage dogs. One is afraid the other will get the start, but we are enough for them any time.

We are close to the city in many places now but there are many bitter weeds grow between us and there. The works of both armies are very near together. They have large forts and so have we. They get to fighting with cannon sometimes, trying to batter down one another's works. Our artillery is too much for them. We soon make them stop and hide their guns. We can shoot to their works with our rifles. They have just commenced fighting with artillery. We are using 8 pieces of cannon. The rebs are using 9, but our boys make the dirt fly around their works and you had ought to hear our boys yell and make fun of them.

They killed and wounded a good many of our men while we were building our works. They had theirs built when we got here and had the advantage of us, but we have got ours built now and it is as fair for us as it is for them, but I am getting sick and tired of the rattle of muskets and cannon night and day all the time now for five months. Not a day has passed over but what we have had more or less of it. I do not know how it would seem to lay down one night and think that I could sleep all night without being routed out and get my gun and cartridge box on, fall into the works and look for the enemy, but less than a year if I live will see my time out. Then I am going to have a good long furlough.

I am the only one of the Gilmanton boys that is with the company now. The others are played out back in hospitals or on detail. Pratt was here this morning. He is camped about two miles from here. He is in the Pioneer Corps. Dan is back with the division train. He is out of all danger, so you need not worry about him. Poor you, if I was you I would make way with Miss Ames.

We have got ten large size guns that the balls weigh sixty-four pounds, shelling the city. They throw one thousand shells every twenty-four hours. The city is nothing but a mass of ruins. It was a splendid place before we commenced shelling it.

We had two visitors day before yesterday. They were Johnny Rebs. They came over and took dinner with us and brought over some corn bread and tobacco and we made some coffee and all sat down on the ground together and had a good chat as well as a good dinner. They gave us some tobacco and we gave them some coffee to take back with them. They stayed about two hours and then went back. They were real smart fellows both of them.

You must not think up there that we fight down here because we are mad, for it is not the case, for we pick blackberries together and off the same bush at the same time, but we fight for fun, or rather because we can't help ourselves. If they would let the soldiers settle this thing it would not be long before we would be on terms of peace, but a few old heads that have got it in their hands and do not have to go in danger will not settle it, or do not want to, for no fear of them losing their lives, and it is filling their pockets with greenbacks.

I had a letter from Thomas Stewart the other day. He is well and sends his respects to you if I heard from you, so I pass his respects right on to you. He is in New Orleans, La. He says he has plenty of fighting as well as the remainder of us. Fight appears to be the general order of the day at the present time.

I had a letter from Mrs. Allen. She said Mr. Allen expected to have to go to the war. It will make the men of Gilmanton look mild when the present draft comes off. War is not half as terrible a thing as one imagines it to be. There is hardly a soldier but what would rather fight than march ten miles. They soon become reckless and do not care for anything no matter what it is.

Well now, I must tell you what we are doing and going to have for dinner. We are going to have minute pudding. We are real stavers to cook. It is cook, yourself, here or starve to death. We propose to prefer the cooking part for our share.

What we are doing is not of much account. We lay here telling what we are going to do when we get home. I am going to Idaho territory to dig gold for two years after I get home. Others are going to stay at home if they live to get there, so they say.

You say Dan may slip up on his intentions, but you must remember that Dan will be a bold soldier boy not to be daunted by trifles, but will have the courage of a sheep and the boldness of a rabbit.

Well, I shall have to close for this time, hoping to hear from you soon and direct as your last. Give my respects to all who you see fit so to do.

Yours truly,
From a Friend,

M. E.   John F. Brobst

CHAPTER FIVE

September 1864–November 1864

"They keep me here"

Atlanta had fallen on September 2, 1864, and there was no doubt as to the effect of this event on the advocates of the Union cause. Politicians, soldiers, and the people at home were now certain of ultimate victory, and some were saying it would come within a few months. Actually, it would be nearly a year before the volunteers would be mustered out and home again, but at least the end was in sight. Sherman's victories in Georgia had shaken the Confederacy. They had strengthened the Republican party and its presidential candidate, Abraham Lincoln, who would be seeking election for his second term. Atlanta was a prize worth fighting for and holding at all costs.

The town itself did not appear to be much of a prize to the Union troops who occupied it. The damage to property had been extensive, and the remaining residents showed evidence of the suffering and sacrifices which they had endured while under siege. Food supplies were already scarce, and the Confederate troops which had evacuated the town were still close enough to interfere with the Union supply lines north of the town. In October, the Twenty-fifth Wisconsin Infantry Regiment accompanied the Seventeenth Corps in an attempt to drive the rebel forces away from the railroad leading from Chattanooga to Atlanta.

John Brobst remained behind. Another attack of malaria had sent him to the hospital, this time to stay for several weeks. John disliked being separated from his friends, but it was impossible for him to accompany them on another march. Illness had left him weak, dizzy, and feverish, and his enthusiasm for army life had deserted him. Fortunately, he was permitted to leave the field hospital at frequent intervals and managed to do some sight-seeing around Atlanta. Meanwhile, he tried to keep track of his regiment's activities and location during October and November, hoping to rejoin it soon.

John had lost Mary's picture, along with those of his sisters, during the battle of July 22 near Decatur, Georgia. Her picture had become a source of comfort; he especially missed it now that he was separated from his friends. Adding to his loneliness was the fact that mail from home stopped coming through soon after he left the regiment. It would be many more months before John received a letter from Mary.

Camped six miles South of
Atlanta Near East Point, Ga.
Sept. the 15th/64

Dear Friend Mary,

It was with great pleasure that I received your ever-
welcome note and was very glad to hear from you and to
hear that you were well, but sorry to hear that you had
lost so near and dear a friend, but we must go sooner or
later, old or young. We are all certain of death at some
time.

My health is not very good at present but better than it
has been. I have been in the hospital for the last ten days
but shall soon join the regt. if I keep on the gain.

The weather is getting quite cool now, and the boys
have begun to feel better and heartier than they did while
it was so very warm.

We are all resting for awhile now. General Sherman
says the campaign is over for a month or six weeks and
we are glad of it. We will probably get paid off here, and
then for more fighting. We will just be about spoiling for
a fight by that time again.

Well, now for the news. I suppose you have heard that
we have got the long sought-for prize, the city of Atlanta.
Well, we have it at last, and lots of real nice things with
it. We got large warehouses full of tobacco, plenty of dry
goods, plenty of everything but money. But the greatest
prizes that we had the good fortune to capture was a fine
lot of secesh war widows and girls, and oh, lots of babies
and little ones of all sizes and colors, ages and looks, fine
looking things, resembling anything from a baboon up or
down to a donkey. The fact of the business is they are a
hard looking nation. They look worse than I used to look

when I had been poorly stayed with when I was up north. But you had ought to see what fools our soldiers are. Those fairs of the south will tell a very pitiful and heart-rending story and the boys must marry them to get them out of their misery. There have been more than fifty weddings now since we have got in here and how many more there will be is more than I can tell. Perhaps you may get catched yourself, Mr. John, your affections are so easily ensnared, but rather think not. No ragamuffin gal can catch this chick. They want more hoops, because it is a Yankee invention, and the nicest fashion they have down here is that of snuff-dipping. The way that it is done, they take a small stick, such a one as they can get into their mouth, and wind a rag around the end of the stick, and wet the rag, then dip it in the snuff and chew it, spit and slobber around just like an old tobacco chewer, and you know how I am down on tobacco chewers.

Today all the women and children must leave Atlanta. All those who have husbands in the rebel army or brothers, fathers, or anyone that they depend on for maintenance, have to go south. It goes against the grain for some of them to go, but old Billy Sherman has said it and go they must, and all those that have got no one to depend on for support in the rebel army are to go north if they choose to go there. If not, south.

There are about twelve thousand women and children in Atlanta, drawing their supplies from the government and we have to be down here fighting their husbands, sons, brothers, and fathers who have run and left them behind for our government to support, but Sherman is bound to send them after their loved lords of southern soil and it is just right in my opinion.

We have plenty of fruit of all kinds here now, apples,

peaches and almost everything that a person can think of
or wish for. There are some of the people that live out in
the country that bring them in and trade them for stuff
that we have and do not want, such as coffee, salt, sugar,
and other small articles that we have and they want.

Well, I shall have to stop writing until after dinner,
for my head aches bad, and then I will write you a little
about our big fight on the first of this month, and on the
fifth, and on the seventh. The rebs came out at the small
end of the horn every time.

Well, now for the first day's fight. In the first place, on
the first day of this month our army began to fall back and
the rebs thought we were retreating, but none but the
20th corps fell back. The balance of our army swung
around to the south, and the first thing that the rebs knew
we were at and in East Point. They had to come out of
their works and fight us. We gave them a hard whipping
then. The only thing that they could do was to leave
Atlanta as soon as possible.[1] We followed them to Jones-
boro. There we came up with them and gave them another and a worse whipping than the first one. Then we
chased them to a place called Rough and Ready. Here we
gave them another whipping and then fell back to East
Point to rest up awhile and get paid off. The rebels lost
very heavy in killed, wounded, and prisoners. Our losses
were light from the fact that we had the choice in the
ground, which is a great advantage in a battle. We took
57 cannon and I do not know how many muskets, 80 cars
loaded with ammunition. We got lots of all kind of ma-
chinery that belonged to the rebel government, and any

[1] The Confederate troops were forced to evacuate, after Sherman
had cut off the only railroad serving the city and threatened to
surround it.

amount of mules and wagons as well as a nice lot of darkies, with many other things too numerous to be mentioned. This is all about the fight.

Well, Mary, you say it seems hard to have so many killed. So it does, but we have the pleasure of knowing that we can and will revenge our brother soldiers. I believe and in fact I know we killed more of the rebs that they do of us. The rebel loss in killed, wounded, and prisoners is thought to be forty thousand since the 15th of July, and I believe it is all of that, if not more, for I have seen the dead rebels lay so thick on the ground that a person could almost walk over the ground on the dead and not step on the ground, and I know that I have seen but a small portion of the rebel dead. We lose men as a matter of course, but I have never seen so many of ours as I have of the rebs. We have lost since the 15th [of] July about twenty thousand killed, wounded, and prisoners, not more than half as many as the rebs.

Well, I think if the Johnny Rebs don't rub me out or shoot an arm or leg off from me, that I will not look much different from what that picture does, only a little more fierce perhaps. As a matter of course, you know, I should look so after hunting men and helping to kill them for three years. Oh, how fierce, are you not almost scared now? Of course you be. I look just as I always did, only I am poor as a shad running down the Susquehanna River in the fall of the year. I think I will have the good fortune to get back all right yet. Only eleven months from today and my time is out, but that is plenty of time to get killed twenty times. But there has never but one rebel ball hit me yet, and that one did not hurt me very bad, not so but what I have gone around all the time.

But the rebs have got your picture, and another one

would do me a great deal of good now. You say I have so many others to look at, but you accuse me wrongfully again, for I have not got any, for the rebs got them all. I had 4, 3 sisters and yours, and that is all that I had.

Well, you say Elsie is well. I had a letter from her. It had all of five lines in it. She wanted to know where Wallace[2] was, and her writing to him all the time and him writing to her. I gave him the letter and let him answer it. Keep this shady you know.

Mary Ames is dead and Dan feels very bad about it. She died the same day that your grandfather[3] did. She had been sick for some time before she died. Chauncey Cooke is sticking around here. Has lost his last good friend from his looks. He wants another furlough. You used him too well when he was up there. He has been good for nothing ever since he got back.

I am glad you are so anxious to hear from me. You are no more so than what I am to hear from you, and I will write as often as you do. And if you fill two sheets I will fill 4, and if you fill 4 I will fill 8. Now that is fair I am sure, is it not?

Well, I shall have to close for this time, hoping to hear from you soon as possible. Tell Curt to play Yankee Doodle on the jawbone, for that is my favorite now. Give my respects to your mother and father and whoever you see fit, and a good portion to yourself. Direct as usual. Yours truly,

A Friend, J. F. Brobst

[2] Private Wallace Wilcox, Gilmanton, Wisconsin, Company G, 25th Wisconsin Infantry Regiment.

[3] Mary's grandfather, Durham S. Inglesby, died at Gilmanton, Wisconsin, in 1864. "Inglesby" is a variant spelling of the family name.

My headquarters in
the hospital yet
Sept. the 26th /64

Well, Mary,

Here I am again writing a few lines to you, but have not
had an answer to my last one, or the last one that is due,
but I shan't send this until I hear from you again, but hope
that will not be very long for I am so lonesome that I do
not know what to do with myself. The doctor will not let
me go to the regt. yet. I had a tumor taken out of my neck,
perhaps you remember it. It is nearly well now and I
think I will soon be allowed to return to my company.

Well, as I was saying, I am lonesome, homesick, and sick
of the war, sick of the south, sick of the north, and sick of
almost everything today, but will feel better by tomorrow,
for we are getting paid off and it will be our turn tomorrow, and it will be the first time that we have been paid
off for over eight months, and we will feel large with over
one hundred dollars in our pockets, worth about forty dollars, but it is all for the Union. Hurrah for Jeff Davis! Not
old Jeff Davis the rebel, but Jeff C. Davis of Indiana, commanding 4th Division, 15th Army Corps, our Jeff.

The news is not of much importance here. The armies
are still laying still. I do not know when they will move.
They are furloughing soldiers home now very fast. I had
the offer of a furlough, but would not take it, and now it
is too late. I did not think that so many of the boys would
get a chance to go home or I should have gone, but if they
let any more go this fall I shall try to get one then, but if
I have no chance to get one this fall again, I will not get
any, for by spring I will not have but a short time to stay,

and will stay my time out and then have a good long one. Thomas Taylor,[4] a brother to the one that was at home last fall, is on his way home. I told him to go to your house and tell you I sent him there to get his dinner and tell you that I was all right.

The rebels captured a train of cars yesterday, the 25th, and burned them up, and did it not two miles from where our forces were encamped, tore up the tracks and left for parts unknown, but the track was all laid and cars running in six hours again. The rebels cut the railroad, but we do not pay any attention to them. Let them undo the work and we do it up again and run our provisions in, and when we get a good supply on hand we will start for them, use them real gently, give them all the lead and iron that they want free of charge. Oh, how liberal we are, good Yankees, are we not? Of course we are all real nice fellows, but we are very bashful at first, but the southern chivalry do not like us because we call Sherman our father and we his boys. They are down on Sherman because he makes them skedaddle for the south.

The general opinion is that we will move in about one month. The boys are all feeling well and want to move again. Sherman is our guide, like Moses of old was guide for the children of Israel, but he did not smite the waters of the Chattahoochee River as Moses did the Red Sea, but we had to wade, swim or roll through it, any way to get through, and when we got out of meat he called for chickens, turkeys, geese, pigs, sheep, and anything that we could take, from the rebs in place of the Egyptians, better

[4] Private Thomas Taylor, Durand, Wisconsin, Company G, 25th Wisconsin Infantry Regiment. His brother was Private Israel Taylor, also in Company G.

than quails. In place of smiting the rock for water, he smites the cellar doors, and the wine, brandy, gin, and whiskey flows in the place of water. Sherman is rather ahead of Moses if he gets us through the wilderness all right, I think.

The horses and mules and cattle are holding a great fair to celebrate the death of the rebel General John H. Morgan.[5] They are singing praise, shouting, braying, running, jumping, and capering at a terrible rate. They think there will be no thief to steal them now for awhile and they feel well over it. McClellan's[6] men are officiating for them. Birds of a feather go together, as the old saying is.

Well, I shall close for today. Will write a little more tomorrow, and a little more the next day, etc.

Sept. the 27th /64

We have had nearly all the prisoners of our regt. that have been taken on this campaign exchanged.[7] They look very bad. They had hard treatment. Not half enough to eat, scarcely any fire to cook what scanty meals they did get, no blankets to keep them warm or any shelter to keep them dry, not even a shade to sit under, but had to lay out in the hot sun and burn. But they did not exchange your picture. I am afraid you are too spunky, and they will be very apt to keep you until the war closes, perhaps place you under fire of our guns, as they have the officers at Charleston. Lord, but I should like to kill the one that has

[5] General John H. Morgan was killed September 4, 1864, at Greenville, Tennessee.

[6] General George B. McClellan, formerly in command of the Army of the Potomac.

[7] Many had been held at Andersonville, Georgia.

that picture if they have it yet. I could kill him with a good heart and clear conscience.

There is considerable excitement here today. The army is nearly all on the move. They commenced last night after I stopped writing. About twenty thousand troops have moved north in the last twelve hours and still keep agoing. There are all kinds of conjectures as to where they are going. Some say back on the railroad, some say to meet the rebel General Forrest, and some say on the Potomac, but nothing certain as to where they are going, but I should rather think they are going on the Potomac, from the fact that it is very necessary to take Richmond before elections. I hope they will get that place soon, for I want to see old Uncle Abe elected again. He is the only man that can settle this war up and do it as it should be settled. If McClellan[8] gets the reins he will have peace sooner than Abe, but by letting them have their slaves. Then we can fight them again in about ten years. But let Old Abe settle it, and it is always settled, is my opinion of the matter.

I expect they are having hot times up north now, the draft coming off and the election too, both at the same time, or so very nearly the same time, and either one would make great excitement from itself, but when it comes to take the two together will make much more than the one alone. I expect they will do some shooting up north as well as down south this fall.

We cannot hear anything about the draft, but the soldier's greatest hope is that old Uncle Abe will enforce the draft right up to the handle, and if he can't do it any other way, let about twenty thousand men go home and

[8] General McClellan was running against Lincoln on the Democratic ticket.

do it for him. We would like to go back and fight northern cowards and traitors than to fight rebels. They are the sole cause of myself and all other soldiers being in the field today. If they had held their tongues we would have all been at home now, but they must blow, and now some of them must fight at home or in the south. They will have their choice, and I hope if they do have to take soldiers home to enforce the draft that I will be one that will have to go, for I could shoot one of them copperheads with a good heart as I could shoot a wolf. I would shoot my father if he was one, but thank God he is not one of the miserablest of all God's creatures, a copperhead, a northern traitor. Very nearly all the soldiers in this department will go for old Abe. If Abe is elected the war will end in about nine months and be eternally ended, and if McClellan is elected it will end in four months for ten years only, is the opinion of every soldier in these parts.

Our regt. has not received marching orders as yet, but cannot tell how soon they may get the order to start. We may not have to go all the way, have the good luck to stay where we are for awhile to guard the rear of our army for awhile. I hope we will, for it is going to be bad to be moving in the fall, out in the cold rains, and no cover or shelter, but stand out like so many cattle and take the storm, but I have stood it for over two years and am in hopes I can stand it the balance of my time out.

Well, those greenbacks have not come around yet, but will be around this afternoon. Then I shall go into the nigger trade I guess. That is the best business of the day, go around and draft niggers and get fifteen dollars for doing it. This is all for this day. I think enough, such as it is. I must clean up my pocketbook. [*Rest of letter missing.*]

Chattanooga, Nov. the 1st, /64

Dear Friend Mary,

I again take the present opportunity of writing to you again, but have not had any answer to the last two that I have written to you, but I have not been with the regiment since I last wrote you, and perhaps that accounts for it, as I always told you to direct to the regiment, and perhaps the Johnny Rebs have got them, as they have been having things their own way down here for the last month or six weeks. They destroyed about thirty miles of the railroad to Atlanta but it is all repaired again. Their object is to compel us to evacuate Atlanta, but I do not think they will succeed now, but we were hard up for provisions at that place. When the railroad was completed our principal living was corn and rice ground up together and then baked into bread, no meat, a very small allowance of coffee, etc. The regt. has been after the rebs all of the time. In fact all of our army and all of the enemy are on the move. Our army has got behind the rebs and are driving them north. They are now in Tenn. They have had several large battles. Our men came off victorious in all except the small posts along the railroad that they overpowered and took the men prisoners of war. Both armies have lived off from the country. The rebels have actually lived on sugar cane for days at a time. This I know to be a fact, for rebel prisoners told me so themselves. The last that I heard from my regiment they were in Larkinsville, Ala., but have since moved on after the rebs and they are headed north, so you must look out up north, for there are breakers ahead. Our Billy Sherman says he is not going to let one of the rebs ever get back south again, but drive them up home and keep the nice little pets, beauties, hom[e].

I have not been able to march since the 25th of August. In hopes of being able soon. All the time I am improving, all the time, but very slowly. But I should go to the regiment now if the doctors would let me go, but I have the promise of going soon. We were taken to Atlanta and stayed there two weeks and then came to this place. We have been here four days. I should have written sooner but could not get a letter through.

There is any amount of conscripts and substitutes passing through this place everyday. There are three thousand of them camped close by as they are waiting for transportation.

I thought the people were going to resist the draft up there, but I see they concluded that old Uncle Abe had too many boys on his side that were not afraid of powder or lead and would like no better fun than to go up there and try our hand with them and make them come. But good for them, they are coming without that trouble. And we are going to have Abe for our next president and then have him call for five hundred thousand more. We want all the copperheads to have a hand in putting down this rebellion. We do not want all the praise, for fear they would be jealous.

The weather is very fine here and has been all the fall so far, and I hope it will continue so all winter, and I think by next spring this war will be played out. The rebs are getting sicker every day of war and they are getting whipped every place badly. And now all we want to close up the game is Abe for President, and then the game is up, the Union saved, and all things will be well with us. If not, then it is divided and our blood spilt for nothing.

This is all the news that I can think of at present, only I am going up on top of Lookout Mountain. You can see into four states from the top of that mountain. It is nearly three miles from the foot to the top. There are three of us going up. I expect we had better stay up there for fear we will never get any nigher heaven again.

I saw Dan about four weeks ago. He was well and hearty, so was Thompson Pratt. Well, I will close for today and perhaps I can write some more after I climb the mountain. I never have been on top of it and shall see some new things no doubt.

Nov. the 2nd. Wet, cold and raining very hard this morning, and has fooled me out of going on the mountain, but [I] shall go some other time when it dries off and the going is better. It is so cold this morning that I can't write very much. I am sitting in a tent almost freezing to death, thinking how close I should embrace the old stove if I was at home, such days as this. But this is the last cold and disagreeable winter for me in the army.

Nov. the 3rd. Still raining and very cold today. I went to town through mud and rain, from the fact that my tobacco ran low, and I might as well be without breath as to be without tobacco, for I should [be] so very cross that the boys would whip [me] to death so I should have to do with[out] either one of the two.

All that I have seen that is new today is eleven thousand refugees that have come in through the mud and rain. They look like the breaking up of the Southern Confederacy after a hard winter. They are mostly all old men, women, and children that could not stay at their homes any longer because they advocated Northern principles. Such is the style of the so-called Southern Confederacy.

Nov. the 4th. Quite pleasant overhead today, but the mud is about one foot deep and that makes it quite unpleasant underfoot. You know, notwithstanding the mud I have been running all over town all day long. Business was very brisk in town today but Uncle Sam monopolizes all. He [has] over two hundred railroad engines in this place at one time. Today they are hurrying in the supplies while they can.

Nov. the 5th. Well, this morning I shall try and finish my letter, as it is Sunday morning. I went out and chopped wood awhile this morning, built a large fire and the[n] commenced writing. This is a cold and windy day as most of the days will be until next May. Soldiers will suffer greatly in this department this winter, as there are no signs of going into winter quarters yet, and probably we will be marching and fighting all winter. My regiment is on the move all the time. I am trying all the time to get back to my Co., but they will not let me go. The old Dutch doctor told me yesterday that better I [j]ust stay here, for the regt. was on a big tramp. They keep me here and about every week I have a shake of the ague and they feed me on quinine and that is all the good it does. Next week I am going to run away and go to the regt., so you can direct to the regt. the same as you always have. When I [get] back to the regt. I shall expect to find your picture.

Well, I believe this is all that I can think of this time, so I shall have to close for the present. Give my respect to your folks and all who you see fit, and a good share to yourself. Nothing more at present, write soon, good-by.

From a friend,

Yours truly, John F. Brobst

Abraham Lincoln of Illinois
For President
Andrew Johnson of Tennessee
For Vice-President

Go away little Mack[9]
You can't come in on this track
We remember Richmond.

[Written up the side of the letter.]

I must write to my sister today. She has got married and is laughing at me because I have to dance in the pig trough, but I will pay her for it today.

[9] General McClellan.

CHAPTER SIX

December 1864–March 1865

"We live in hopes"

John Brobst never did get back to his regiment during the winter of 1864–65. He was still in Chattanooga when the Twenty-fifth Wisconsin Volunteers returned to Atlanta on November 11, and within a few days they had left again without him. This time they were off on a long march across Georgia to the sea, with General Sherman. All during the winter months that followed they kept moving through the forests, swamps, and streams of Georgia and South Carolina, while John was still standing

99

guard duty back in Dalton. They were tearing up railroad tracks and burning southern property with a vengeance, while John had trouble gathering enough news to write a letter home.

As the distance between John and his regiment widened, he despaired of ever seeing his friends again. They were leaving no lines of supply or communication behind them, and the possibility of his ever catching up with them appeared increasingly remote. John's long convalescence seemed to have cost him almost more than it was worth.

In January of 1865, John and other soldiers belonging to the Army of the Tennessee who had been separated from Sherman's command by reason of furloughs or convalescence, were serving together in a provisional division under General T. F. Meagher in Tennessee. While they waited and wondered what their next assignment would be, General Grant was making plans for them. They were soon to be transferred, along with additional troops under General John M. Schofield, to a port in Maryland, from which they would embark for North Carolina by sea. There they would gather at Beaufort and New Bern, which were now held by the Union, and wait for General Sherman's army which was marching northward through the Carolinas. When Sherman reached Goldsboro, they would all join forces for the final effort which was necessary to end the Civil War.

John was with Meagher's division in Chattanooga when it was ordered to move east. The journey would be long and unpleasant by riverboat, boxcar, and ocean steamer, but when John realized that he might be reunited with his regiment in North Carolina, he knew the whole miserable trip could be endured.

John eagerly looked forward to seeing his friends again. He had heard nothing from them for months and was anxious to know all about their march to the sea with Sherman. He also hoped that his mail would soon reach him again, as he had received no letter from Mary since September. By the end of March, things would look much brighter for John, and life would once more be worth living.

[Dalton, Georgia
December 11, 1864]

[*Beginning of letter missing.*]

December the 11th

After I got my dinner yesterday, I went to bed and took a good nap and did not write any more that day, but shall write some today. Shall not promise how much or how interesting, so here goes, let the writing tell for itself.

This morning is cold and gloomy and getting colder all the time. I am on picket today. Perhaps I will have the pleasure of seeing a reb or two. If I do see any, I shall certainly pay my compliments to them in the shape of powder and lead. Well, I will close until I come off picket. Perhaps I can see or hear something that will interest you somewhat.

December the 12th

Off picket this morning once more. One time less to stand guard down in Dixie. Last night was a horrid cold night. It cleared off yesterday and grew cold all day long. The

wind blew a perfect hurricane all day and all night and
froze the ground quite hard. Ice is about one and a half
inches thick. Nothing happened of any note on guard last
night, only a poor rebel cow came up to the line without
the countersign, and the boys would show her no mercy,
but shot her and we had to dress her and carry her to camp,
and it came in very good play as we are on half rations at
present.

I can't think of anything to write, for I am just as homesick as I can be, and have been for the last ten days. No
news, no letters, no nothing to pass away time with. Eight
months and two days yet, and then comes a day of thanks-
giving and rejoicing for me, if I am all safe and sound yet.
When that time comes, I shall begin to think strongly of
getting home all right, fat, ugly, ragged, and saucy. Well, I
will close for today. Goodbye for this lonesome day.

Not quite done for this day after all. I had a visitor this
afternoon, Captain Kinian,[1] the captain in charge of this
battalion, was in here talking and telling me of his adventures in the Rocky Mountains and in California. He has
got the Idaho fever and wants me to go with him as soon
as our time is out. He has almost given me the gold fever
too, but I have got enough on my hands for the present.

Well, here comes an old soldier a chum of mine and I
shall have to stop for today.

December the 13th

All passed off quiet today until about two o'clock this
afternoon, and then it was all excitement. About twenty-
five rebels came up to picket line and frightened the recruits, as well as the officers, nearly out of their wits. A

[1] No record of a captain by this name, probably misspelled.

few shells soon dispersed them and we have about one hundred cavalry after them. We have had no cavalry here until today. One hundred came in, just in time to go out after the rebs. They make their appearance on some high bluffs similar to the bluffs in Gilmanton, so that they can be seen a long way off, but dare not venture up very close. Dalton is situated in a valley similar to Buffalo Valley. A high range of hills and mountains all around it gives it a natural fortified position. We have quite a good fort and four pieces of artillery in the fort and about twelve hundred men at the present time. It is a very cold day today, uncommonly cold for this country. This is all for today. Perhaps tomorrow will bring forth a day of glad tidings and great joy. Goodnight.

December the 14th

Nothing of importance today. The best word today is I am full of hopes with but little patriotism. This is a very fine day, the sun shines warm and nice. It is washing day, cold lunch for dinner, etc. And eight months from today to serve Uncle Sam. Then I hope to be at liberty once more. I tell you I count the days close about now. If I was with the regiment it would not be so lonesome. This is all for the 14th day of December.

December the 15th

Today I have been hard at work all day, tearing down buildings and destroying property generally, for that is the way that we carry on the war now, raze, burn, and destroy everything we come to.

Two years ago tonight I stayed all night at your house, but tonight I will probably stay at Dalton, Ga. Two years ago this morning, you filapeaned me, and about eight months from today, it will be my turn, so you must keep it in your mind, for I certainly will be the winner the next time.

December the 16th

Today it is raining as usual. Gloomy day today for me. I am sitting in my mansion today, with magnificence and luxury in the shape of beef bones, hard tack, and a plug of tobacco laying on the window jamb. This constitutes the luxuries of a soldier.

I had quite a dream last night. I dreamed that I had two visitors, and they were no other than Mary Englesby and her mother who come to see how soldiers had their household furniture arranged, and laughed at me then, after I took so much pains to show you all over the house, up garret, down cellar and all around. Well, this is all for today, only I am boiling a pot of beef today. I wish, hurrah here, over goes the kettle, beef and all, put out the fire and discombobligated things generally. Now I shan't write another bit today. Everything is upside down, wife scolding, young ones squalling, dogs howling, and myself provoked, so goodbye until I get a little composed.

December the 17th

Well, today I am in some better humor than I was yesterday. The news is good today. We have the news today that Thomas has defeated Hood[2] with the loss of one thousand men prisoners and sixteen pieces of artillery. This

[2] Generals George H. Thomas and John B. Hood. This refers to the Battle of Nashville, resulting in decisive defeat of Hood's Confederate army.

is good news if it only proves true, and I think it is true. Now I hope they will open communications and then you will get this nonsense. Today is wet and disagreeable as usual. Georgia is a very pleasant place for them that take a fancy to it, but I had rather live on Beef Slough Island[3] than down here, and it is the meanest place I ever was in up north. Well, last night, Phillips, a Sheboygan man and myself were keeping livery stable up in Wisconsin, making money like dirt. This is all today.

Sunday, December the 18th

Today is the Lord's day, but I shall steal a few moments to write to you. Last night, I heard that Thomas had taken forty-six pieces of artillery and three thousand prisoners, but it is too good to be true, so I shall not put much dependence in the report, but if true, so much for the better for us. That means you and me and every man, woman, and child up north. Phillips and I have been keeping livery stable for two days now and have not made a dollar yet, but we are going to make money when our horses get back, for they are all let out now, for I cannot find one of them on the premises. It is quite warm and pleasant today, all except the mud, and is delicious as a matter of course. Well, Christmas will soon be here and I will be here too. At least, I expect to be. I hope you will have a good time. As for myself, all I expect is a soldier's Christmas, that is a feast on hard tack and coffee, short allowance at that, but if I live to see another Christmas and New Year, I hope I shall see them pass off in Wisconsin once more. Well, I shall have to close for today and go to the depot and get a paper. The train has just come in from Chattanooga, so good day.

[3] Near Alma, Wisconsin.

December the 19th

Nothing of great importance today. Nothing has tran-
spired today except small camp rumors. All kind of stories,
but none of any importance. It is a kind of a disagreeable
day as usual, raining some. Just enough to keep it very
muddy and unpleasant.

December the 20th

Well, Mary, today we have good news, if it is only true.
The news is Thomas has defeated and completely routed
Hood. If it is only true, it will be a good thing, both for the
soldiers posted here and for the glorious cause that we are
here to establish and protect. Every breeze brings news of
victory for the cause of the Union and I hope it will continue so until the last foul traitor is made to bite the dust
in the agonies of death. I do not see how they can hold out
much longer. They are defeated everywhere. Nothing but
foolhardiness causes them to hold out as long as they have.
No men of sound sense can or would hold out in a war that
is bringing desolation to them, and them only. But it is hard
to tell what the fools will do. If we must exterminate them,
then we must, for the flag will, must and shall float over
every foot of territory that the traitors claim as a southern
confederacy. But I hope it will be soon a cry of peace in-
stead of defeat or victory on either side. Well, this is all for
today. Goodnight.

December the 21st

No news from Thomas since yesterday and this is a very
cold day. It is snowing a very little. It rained very hard all
night last night and this morning the wind got in the north
and sends us some of the fresh and keen air from the land
of ice and snow. By the way, I heard from a drafted man

here that H. N. Muzzy was drafted. Oh, is not that right-eous, if he had only had to come himself! And I heard that Lunderville was drafted.[4] I have a little pity for him, but none for H. N., not in the least. Good day.

December the 22nd

Well, Mary, here is another long, cold, and lonesome day to wear away at something, what I do not know. I have killed some time talking with a rebel deserter. He stayed with me last night. His name is James Brown. He is a very clever fellow. He is tired of war and has escaped and got safely inside of our lines. He is going home in a day or two. He lives in Tenn. He will stop a day or two with me yet. We have some friendly talk about the battles we have been in. We have been hotly engaged against one another several times. The 22nd of July[5] was one day. We have talked the scenes of that day all over several times since he has been here. He and I are going over town today so I must bid you good morning.

December the 23rd

Well, Mary, I have something strange to tell you this morning. Yesterday, this James Brown and I got to talking about the girls as a matter of course. I told him I thought the northern girls were the handsomest and while we were talking he told me he had pictures of four northern girls. At least, he supposed they were, for he got them the 22nd of July. I wanted to see them, so he let me see them, and it was your picture, with my three sisters. I told him so,

[4] No record of H. N. Muzzy. Private Andrew Lunderville of Gil-manton, Wisconsin, was with Company K, 25th Wisconsin Infantry Regiment.

[5] The Battle of Atlanta.

and it was some time before I could make him believe it, but I told him all that there was in the knapsack that had them in, so he gave them back to me. I tell you I was glad to get them. They have been kept very nice, just as nice as I could have kept them myself and done my best, and the result is I have been taking a long look at you this morning. I told Brown what you had written to me, that you wished you had ahold of him and you would show him what a northern girl could do. He laughed and wants me to tell you that he sends his best respects and that he has carried you in his coat pocket five months and you were docile and gentle as a lamb, never found a word of fault. He is going home this evening. This is all for today. Good-by until tomorrow and Christmas, for it is almost here.

Sunday, December the 25th, Christmas at that

Well, Mary, I wish you a Merry Christmas. I hope you will have a good time, go to a good ball and have a nice, handsome beau with a heart as large as an ox liver, a fast horse, a nice cutter, and no whiskey. Well, the people are big old-time[r]s up north at sleighing parties. Just the thought of it makes me unhappy. Only think what times, with a fast trotter, a nice little cutter just large enough for two, plenty of buffalo robes, plenty of bells, plenty of snow, and a gay handsome girl by one's side. Two forty on the plank, let her went!

Well, I came off picket this morning and have had a gay old dinner, a loaf of corn bread [and] a chicken that cost enough to be good. I baked the bread myself, boiled my chicken awhile, stuffed it with corn meal and hard tack, potatoes, onions, salt, pepper and pork grease, and put it in a bake kettle, roasted it some, fried it some and burnt it some, and taking it all together, you see I had several chickens—a boiled chicken, a stewed chicken, a fried chicken, a roasted chicken, a baked chicken and a burnt chicken. Some roasted-up, stewed-up, fried-up, baked-up and cooked-up nasty little oysters, and a cup of coffee, all for a Christmas dinner down in Dixie.

I am going over town and get a jew's harp and play and dance, call off, and be the musician, landlord, landlady, and party all myself. Well, there is no news here. The same thing over every day, and I have written nonsense enough for one day at least, so good-by for today.

December the 26th
Nothing of much importance today. I feel somewhat sleepy after my Christmas spree. I went to a real secesh ball last night, lots of rebel girls to dance with and gas with. We had four fiddles and about sixty couples. We could dance four sets in the hall and had a very good time considering where it was, way down south in Ga.

Fifteen citizens drew guns and ammunition today and went out in the country to defend their homes. The rebs drove them in here, and they say the rebs are starving their families to death and they will defend their homes or die. Good for them.

December the 27th
Nothing new today, raining like smoke as usual. It is getting so very muddy that we can hardly get around at all. I am just about as lonesome as I can very well be. I am sick and tired of this place, but expect I will be more so before I get a chance to leave it. I could send this small letter off this morning, but I shall wait until after New Year and then send it so as to have it as long as possible, to try your patience as much as possible.

Last night the patrol guards arrested almost all of our

officers and put them in the lockup. They had got too much noisy whiskey and had to be taken care of. They are very nice birds playing checkers with their noses through the iron grates. It will teach them to take a good joke.

December the 28th

Today it is more pleasant, sun shining, very pleasant. Looks something like home this morning, quite cold but very clear. All the news that happened here, happened with those fifteen men that I told you went out to their homes. They had a small fight with ten or twelve rebs, killed two of the rebs and mortally wounded another. One of the citizens was slightly wounded. They have built them a small fort and intend to hold it. I hope they will.

We have good news from all forts. General Thomas has completely routed the rebel General Hood. General Sherman has taken Savannah and the rebellion is fast playing out. I think by the time that my time is out the war will be over. But the best news is Lincoln has called for three hundred thousand more to fill the places of the runaways. I guess the people will soon find out it will be for their interest to watch all drafted men and see that they do not run away and leave others in the limbos, and have to go in the place of some other man that has run away and is not fit to be an American citizen, and a disgrace to all American citizens.

December the 31st

Well, Mary, we pass over the few days from the 28th to 31st as there is nothing of any importance. We will bury them in the tomb of time as we have done with many days of greater note. There is nothing of importance today, but it is the last day of the year. The old year will soon be gone forever. How many have gone to their long homes since one year ago today. Gay and happy one year ago today, but as sixty-four passes off in the sea of time it finds them mouldering in their cold graves. Many of my comrades that were well and promising one year ago, today sleep under the soil of Georgia, but they have filled a hero's grave. They sleep in honor of their country, and all friends to our government should feel proud of their mouldering bodies. But how many look on them with disdain and say, "He was nobody but a soldier. We will enjoy the rights that he died for. We care not who suffers death for the good of the country. We will undo all that they can do." But the day is fast coming when such men will have to curtail the cowardly and unruly tongues that hang in their heads or they will fill a grave more degrading than that of a soldier. Yes, a grave of disgrace and shame, a Benedict Arnold grave, the grave of a traitor.

Well, we will close for this evening with the [old] year, and begin in the morning with the new year.

January the 1st, 1865

Good morning, Miss Englesby. I wish you a Happy New Year, a good time today, and hope every day of the year will crown you with pleasure and happiness, and no sorrow enter the door of your heart, not only for this year but for all time to come. I hope your path will be strewn with roses and not with thorns. As for me, I do not pretend to know how it will be. My life is a soldier's life and its current never runs smooth. We take hardship when it comes with vigor, and happiness when it merely flickers in the distance, for the good word happiness never approaches us very closely, but we take it as it comes and thank God that it is no worse. I shall stay in my shanty all day today and think of the good times gone by and let the future take care of itself. Take danger when it comes and laugh at it when it passes away, and talk of it in after days. I have been looking at your picture this morning. It looks natural as life when I last saw you, but you have no doubt changed since I last saw you. There was a chum of mine came in the tent while I was looking at you and he must see you then as a matter of course. He gave you a very good compliment. He says you are handsome. Good for him. He is not the only one that thinks so, but I do not want to flatter you nor do not mean it as flattery, and you must not take it as flattery, for you are apt to think everything [I] say is meant in light, but it is not the case. I talk fairly with you. [*Rest of letter missing.*]

Camp Near New Bern, N.C.
February the 21st/65

Dear Friend Mary,

I again occupy a few moments of leisure to write you a few lines to inform you of my whereabouts. I am at or near New Bern, North Carolina. We arrived here on the 8th of the present month. Have been very busy building quarters and are getting along fine. My squad has got ours completed and are living in it. It is a small log hut with a cloth roof, chinked up and corked up with moss, makes it quite comfortable this time of the year. The weather is fine, warm and pleasant for early spring.

The country is very poor, no better than it is around Black River Falls,[6] and that is the poorest part of God's

---

[6] Black River Falls, Wisconsin.

creation that I ever expected to see. Plenty of colored population, but white ones are rather scarce in these parts. Negroes, white sand, and scrub pine constitutes what I have seen of North Carolina.

We had a very hard and cold time in getting here. I was glad when our journey was at an end for a short time. I do not know how long we will remain here, but it is supposed we will stay here some time. There is one thing very evident, that is we will tarry here until we go away. On my way here I passed within twenty-five miles of where my sisters live.[7] I wanted to stop and go and see them real bad, but could not go unless I wanted to be called a deserter, and I had rather suffer death than be stamped and called a deserter.[8] We came through Indiana, Ohio, Penn., Maryland, and Virginia to get here, making in all nineteen states I have been in, within the last two and a half years. I wrote to my sisters and told them how close I was, and how little good it did me, but there is a better time coming, perhaps, for me with others. Perhaps not for me, but for others. Someone will see better times at least.

The hardest time that I have seen since I left Dalton, Ga. was after I embarked on an ocean steamer. We had a very heavy gale and I was so seasick that I could not hold myself up, and nearly all the boys were sick, some praying, some singing, some swearing.

We have plenty of oysters here. All that we have to do is go down on the beach and pick them up and open the

[7] In Ohio.

[8] Other men in John's division may not have had any qualms about deserting. According to official records, General Meagher reported having 7,000 troops in his division when it left Nashville, and only 3,000 after its arrival in North Carolina.

shell, and you have them all nicely dressed. M. R. Bump,[9] a sargt. in my Co., and myself went down and opened them, until we found that it was the cheapest to hire some black man to open the next that we wanted. It is quite a curiosity to see an oyster bed. They grow in very large bunches, sometimes two or three dozen in a bunch.

We have not reached our commands yet, and it is hard to tell when we will, but we live in hopes, perhaps die in despair, but rather think not. We will stand the storm. It won't be long, we will anchor bye and bye.

I have been washing today again, and had it all out by 9 o'clock. Do you not think I would make a smart housekeeper? I think I would, but self-praise won't go very far.

We are formed in a provisional division, Army of the Tennessee, under General Mayer,[10] and will remain here until our commands gain some point so that we can get to them. At present they are in the interior of South Carolina, and cannot tell when we will get to them, but I hope soon, for we cannot get any mail, or have not as yet, but the General says we can get it here. I have not had a letter since last September yet, and I can't hardly write any, for I do not know but I am intruding on the feelings of the persons who I write to. Perhaps this is the case with you, but I hope not. If it should be the case, let me know.

All the drafted men and substitutes have been taken out and sent to the front. The reason why it was done I cannot tell. There is no news to write. We are away back from the front and cannot hear or see anything. All we see is our precious selves and all we hear is camp gossip. Churn it all up and it amounts to just an 0. We will prob-

[9] Sergeant Mensus R. Bump, Mondovi, Wisconsin, Company G, 25th Wisconsin Infantry Regiment.

[10] General T. F. Meagher.

ably stay here two or three months and that will give us ample time to get mail from home once more, and we will rejoice when such a time comes. [*Rest of letter missing.*]

Camp Chattanooga, New Bern, N.C., March 1st/65
Provisional Division, Army of Tenn.

Friend Mary,

Having a day of leisure, and thinking perhaps you would be pleased to hear from me, hoping so at least, I will write to you, although there is not much news to write.

Perhaps I embarrass you by writing so often. If so, I hope my presumption will be pardoned. I hope you will inform me if you wish to end this corresponding that we have been having. Sometimes I think that the reason that I do not get any mail from you is simply because you do not write. If this should be the case please let me know it. If not, do not deem me chastising you, for this is not the case. I only feel anxious to hear from you. I wrote to you a few days ago and am writing again without any answer to several of my last.

There is not much news here to write. They are having a very lively time here today over the news. I glory in the news, but am taking no part in the excitement of the day. Brass bands and drums, fifes playing. Firing cannon, muskets, rifles, and revolvers until the earth fairly trembles while I am sitting in my tent and writing to you.

Charleston and Wilmington are both taken, with a large amount of government property. The last seaport to the Confederacy is forever sealed. Speculation runs high today as well as whiskey. Some of the officers are going around offering to bet from five hundred to five thousand dollars that the war will close in March, but I can't see it in that light, Although I really hope it will, I think I will have the displeasure of serving my time out if I live.

I have five months and thirteen days more to stay in the service of Uncle Sam. Time seems to pass slower now than it ever did. Everything seems to go wrong. Not a letter for seven months, and not knowing when I will get one.

I will try and compose a few lines, as I have nothing else to do. Shall not promise how good they will be, as I have never composed a verse in my life, but here goes, and you must not show them to anyone but yourself. Laugh at them but do not let others laugh at me.[11]

I am well and hope you are the same. My respects to you and your folks.

John F. Brobst

New Bern, N.C., March the 1st/65
Camp Chattanooga

Hurrah, hurrah, have you heard the news,
Old Jeff Davis has surely got the blues,
For this man of wisdom and wonderful renown
Has just discovered the Confederacy going down.

It was but the other day our Sherman did call
At the head of his columns, for Columbia to fall.
To this they quickly and wisely complied,
But we have no doubt that they were mortified.

Oh, Sherman, oh, Abraham, they eagerly say,

[11] John's poem is far from laughable, and it contains a surprising amount of information.

We know we have been humbugged and wandered away,
For Jeff Davis, Floyd, and many others, indeed,
Told us we were wronged, so we thought we would secede.

And we have seen our folly as many other fools do,
We know we can do no better than surrender our all up to you.
Hardee, sworn to defend us or in this city we should dig him
    his grave,
But he soon bethought him his own traitorous being to save.

And now the people of Charleston are also in fear,
For the columns of Sherman are fast drawing near.
The fate of Branchville and Columbia it truly will share
And Sherman his base of supplies will make there.

And then for Richmond his famed army will go
And join our Grant and that city lay low.
This will take time as all other things do,
Nevertheless Sherman and Grant will put the thing through.

Since I began these lines to write,
The soldiers are shouting with all their might,
For news has come, if only true
Our hard times will surely soon be through.

The news has come through a reliable source
That Sherman has taken Charleston by force.
Wilmington, too, they really do say,
Surrendered to General Terry the other day.

They now intend to arm their poor slaves,
Their doomed Confederacy merely to save.
Those blacks come in from far and near
To freedom's land, for they know 'tis dear.

This much we have gained without any fight,

For our cause is honorable, just and right.
To our God we give up all our trust,
And in him conquer, surely we must.

This so-called Confederacy is crumbling away,
And still it grows weaker day after day.
A few more months of hardship and toil,
These traitors' foul schemes forever we will foil.

There is Johnston and Bragg, their mettle we have tried.
We have taken Atlanta and Rome, although strongly fortified,
And many other places too numerous to mention,
Have been deserted by the approach of Sherman's brave
    legion.

There is Hardee brave, though we know that he runs,
From the fact he cannot stand the crack of our big guns.
The most of those men mentioned we have had the pleasure to
    see
And the remainder of our attention we will turn unto Lee.

Although he has deemed it expedient of late
To remove his supplies and Richmond evacuate,
For fear his band of ragamuffins he'll lose,
At least if I mistake not, so says the news,

Soon, soft peace will spread her wings and glide sweetly o'er,
And the thunder of battle will cease to roar.
Then proudly marching homeward we will come,
For we have saved the land bequeathed to us by Washington.

We long for home and its charm so dear.
Oh, there we feel that our loved friends are near,
And in the paths of truth and virtue to keep,
Our ever-wayward, wandering feet.

There is one I know is ever dearer far to me
Than all this wide world can ever, ever be.
I hope we may once more meet,
And never another cruel parting greet.

Oh, how near and yet how far apart
Far on the surface of the earth, but near unto my heart
No matter how far on earth I chance may be
My heart, fair one, is ever yet with thee.

[*Written up the side of two pages of the poem.*]

>   I would not live always, even if I could,
>   But I need not worry, for I couldn't if I would.

Write as soon as possible. Address Co. C, 3rd Batt., 2nd
Brig., Prov. Div. A.T.
Good by for the present. Yours as ever,

>   John F. Brobst

>   Camped near Goldsboro, N.C.
>   March the 27th/65

Dear Mary,

  I take these few moments of leisure to answer your kind
and more than welcome letter. It was the first that I have
heard from you for six months, and how long those months
seemed to be. It seems like an age, but yours of the seventeenth of February is at hand, and words that it contains I
would not have changed for worlds like this.

  Twelve hours ago I felt different than I do at this moment. I knew that you alone could promote my happiness

or seal my misery forever, but thank the kind Providence, you have chosen the former. Mary, I am contented now I know you are true. I have no more fears, no more thoughts of mistrust, no more doubts in my mind. The great gulf has passed and may the stream of life glide smooth and sweetly on until we can meet once more. Meet, I hope to part no more until grim death with his ghostly message summons one or the other to go. Then we must answer to his call. We must then leave all that is dear to us, but only for a short season.

I cannot express my feelings. Words cannot express them. Suffice it to say that I swear by All Above to prove true to you. Nothing can change my mind. My whole affections hover around you. There the wings of my roving and unsettled mind can fold in contentment and confidence, and trust no change of body can change my mind. The noble heart beats as warmly and as affectionate as ever. Think no more of flattery, come in your mind no more. Do not wrong me for one instant with such thoughts. All, all I desire is the same confidence in me that I have in you.

I do not blame you for mistrust when such talk as that passes from the lips of another. What grounds she[12] has to use such language as that I cannot tell. God knows that I never entertained any such a thought, and if she says that I ever mentioned any such thing as marriage to her any other way than joking before all the family, she certainly speaks false as the demon himself. If I live to get back I can satisfy you from her own letters that are in my possession now, that were written one year ago. Since that time I have not written her a single note, but have received six from her, and you can judge what any sensible

---

[12] Mary's Aunt Elsie.

person would do in a case of that kind. Six letters and no answer, I should think she would stop talking. But Mary, let her talk. Pay no attention to her. She could never be a wife of mine if she was the last woman on the face of God's footstool, no never.

Tell me all. You shall be nearest to my heart at all times, in danger or times of hardship or when sitting on the cold and chilly bosom of Mother Earth with her soft sweet breath flitting over solitary, rough, but welcome bed of ease. You are the first in my mind in times of danger. Last, when I cease to breathe. Do not fear to trust me for a moment. Place your confidence in me just as I do in you. I do not ask any more. It would be unjust in me to ask any more, but that is sufficient.

Mary, if I had known what I know now I should have been home on furlough long ago, but if kind Providence permits me to escape for the next four months I shall entertain strong hopes of returning in safety. Oh, how I want to see you. I could tell of adventures to interest you, and talk on other subjects as well.

The present that I am going to send you the first opportunity that I can get it will be a ring, a token of the love I have for you, with my miniature in it. I would have got it, but I did not know that you would accept it, and now as I know that you will, the first opportunity that presents itself I will send it, get it set with a case over the top similar to a locket. As soon as we get where I can get the ring I will do so.

I thought you were surely offended at my blind confidence to take the liberty to write that large letter to you, and my presumption on the half sheet of paper. From the fact that I could not hear from you sometimes, I thought that you were agoing to deny me your friendship, but forgive this one act of injustice and I shall never be guilty of another thought of injustice to you.

I wanted to write to you time after time, but not knowing what might be the result, I did not very often, and when I did write I was reluctant to send it, not knowing but you had rather not hear from me, but let the past be forgotten and look in the future for brighter and happier days. I certainly shall win the filapean, and then I want to ask the privilege of officiating in regard to what the present shall be. One thing and one thing only can pay the debt, and you cannot purchase the present with all the gold in Christendom. Yet you have it and can give it if your heart goes with it. The present is your hand for life.

Now I will tell you what little news I can gather up. In the first place, I have had the pleasure of rejoining my regt. and Co., where I can get some mail. I joined them on the 25th of this month.

We had some very hard fighting before we got to the regt. On the 8th, 9th, and 10th of this month we were fighting at Kinston,[13] and Sherman was fighting at Fayetteville. We, that is, where I was, our loss was about fifteen hundred killed, wounded, and prisoners all included. The loss of the enemy was about thirty-five hundred. They charged our works, and were repulsed with heavy loss in killed and wounded.

I have not much news to write from the fact that I do not hear any news. Sherman's raid was a complete success all through, and I am in hopes that one more raid will close the rebellion.

Dan and Thompson are well and hearty as well as myself, and I hope you are the same. The weather is very

[13] Under General J. D. Cox.

pleasant for the last few days but the month of February and the first part of March was very wet and disagreeable. I hope the wet part of the season is over.

I will write to you every week when I am where I can, and I hope you will do the same for me, and if you do not hear from me as often as once a week, you must not think I have forgotten you, for that will never be the case. I hope you will write too, as often as once a week, even if you should not hear from me that often, for when we are on a campaign we cannot send off any mail, and I shall be glad to hear from you [as] often as possible.

I will send you one dollar and want you to send me a half dollar's worth of stamps and keep the others for yourself. We cannot get any here and I am almost out. I must stop and eat my dinner.

Well, dinner [is] over. I will finish my letter, but it is about finished now, for the mail is going out in a few moments, so I shall have to close for this time. Give my respects to your father and mother and my love to you alone. Write soon, address to the regt. and Co. Yours forever, good-by for this time.

John F. Brobst

P. S. Be sure and put 1st Division, 17th A. C.[14]

[14] Part of Sherman's Right Wing (Army of the Tennessee) under General O. O. Howard.

CHAPTER SEVEN

April 1865–May 1865

"We have whipped them"

The Twenty-fifth Wisconsin Volunteers had just one more march to go before the end of the war, and this one would be neither long nor difficult. They would march from Goldsboro to Raleigh, where they were to wait for a possible order from General Sherman to start fighting, if the Confederate General Johnston refused to surrender. Lee had surrendered his army to Grant on April 9, but his surrender did not include Confederate troops under other commands. It would be up to Sherman either to negotiate with Johnston or to fight one more decisive battle. As Sherman rode out to meet Johnston, his troops stood in readiness, willing to settle the matter by force if necessary.

Sherman met with Johnston at a small farmhouse near Raleigh on April 17, 1865. Both generals had hoped for a speedy settlement without further bloodshed; but now a new factor would have to be considered. They had just received word that Abraham Lincoln was the victim of a tragic assassination plot, apparently planned by a fanatic group of Southern sympathizers. Lincoln's death would be a loss felt by the whole country, which was now badly in need of his steadying influence and sense of justice.

In the interest of a just peace, it was now clearly urgent that Sherman and Johnston reach an agreement before Northern sentiment was further inflamed by news of Lincoln's death. They quickly drew the broad outlines of a plan to terminate the war and restore peace to North and South. However, in their desire to cover all phases of transition from war to peace, they included a number of matters which were not within their jurisdiction. When the agreement was sent to Washington for approval, it was immediately rejected amid loud complaints that the South was being treated too well. General Sherman was heaped with abuse, and General Grant came to Raleigh from Washington in order to supervise personally the surrender of General Johnston. The terms finally agreed upon were similar to those given General Lee.

During the week which elapsed before the second agreement was signed, the soldiers in Sherman's army grew restless and bitter over the treatment given to their beloved "Uncle Billy" Sherman by the politicians in Washington. They remained loyal to him, ready to defend all his actions, right or wrong.

But now the end of the war was at last a reality, and nothing was more important to the soldiers than the prospect of beginning their homeward march. John Brobst was more eager than ever to be on his way. Mary had given him reason to believe that her love would be his alone, and at the moment nothing could have meant more to a homesick volunteer. The task which had taken him so far from Gilmanton was almost over.

Camped near Goldsboro, N.C., April the 2d/65.
Sunday

No letter from you since I last wrote you.

Dear Mary,

I again take the present opportunity of writing a few lines to you to fulfill my promise in my last. My health is good as usual. Hope yours is the same.

I have not much news to write. There is not much stir here, except the stir that naturally arises from getting ready for another campaign. All is in [a] bustle in that way. The cars are running very briskly, bringing in supplies of all kinds for us. I think there will be a forward movement soon, from the appearance. Sherman says there is no rest for his army as long as this rebellion lasts. We begin to think so at present, although I have not had as hard times in regard to marching as the other boys in my Co. for I have not been with them on the last two long marches, but I should like to see them that have been on the march have a little rest.

There is some talk that the Army of the Tennessee will remain along the coast and do garrison duty, but I shall not believe it until we get the order to stay.

There are a few rebels lurking around here, but not enough of them to do themselves any good, or us any harm—merely scouting parties who dare not come very close. They do not love the whistle of balls much better than I do, and that is not very well, I assure you.

This will probably be the last tramp for us, as we only have four months and twelve days to stay. We will soon be one hundred days men. How glad I shall be when my time is out. Then I shall be on hand and wake you long sleepers up, for it must be lonesome up there, for all the young men are all gone, and if the young ladies are anything like me, it would be rather dull to have my own sex only to talk with, but all are not like me. It would be a strange world if they did.

This is Sunday, and it is a lonesome day for me. Plenty of company, but not the right stripe to suit me. I am sitting in my tent all alone, no one to bother me. All the boys are sitting around in the sun, speculating on the war, and as soon as I get through writing to you, I will go out and join the ring.

It is a very pleasant day. The sun shines very warm and pleasant. And I have your picture lying on the stand before me and I kissed it. Oh, how I wish I was in Gilmanton today. I bet I would kiss the original or tip over, as someone else did better than two years ago. Perhaps you know who and where and how it was. If you don't I do, and if I had been Daniel I should never have given it up in that way. I surely should have had the kiss or I should have been trying to get it yet sure as the world. If it had been me I should have been considered a deserter unless you gave me the kiss. Oh, I am all spunk on that line. If talking made folks brave, how brave I could be. Why I would not fear anything in the world, but talk is the smallest portion of it.

I have got some verses in this delicate little letter that were composed by a member of the 18th Wis. Vol. on Sherman's marches. I think they are quite good. There is nothing in this world like Sherman's army.

Daniel had quite a laugh at my expense last night. He told the boys about my coming after the rattlesnake oil that summer that I enlisted. Perhaps you remember it, but he tells it to suit himself. He declares that I did not want the oil, and it was only an excuse that I got up because he was there. So the boys have it the way he tells it, and pay no attention to the way I tell it. But we must have some fun and it might as well be at my expense as at any others. Little did Dan or even Mary know my thoughts those days. I flatter myself that myself was the only one that did know them in this world. I thought, "Daniel, I will let you alone now, but in two or three years from now, we will see who will win the prize."

Proud spirit of man, I used to think that person never did or ever would live that I could be willing to say that [I] loved better than a sister, but there is one in spite of all that kind of thoughts and I am proud to say that I love better than a sister, and that one is you, Mary. I hope you will not fear to place your confidence in me any longer, for you certainly must admit that I place all my confidence in you, and if I did not, surely I should not write to you as I do.

If we march from here they may not keep communications open and if they do not I cannot send you any letters until they do, and Mary, do not think that I have forgotten you for one moment. No, Mary, you are never out of my mind, let what may come, yet I will, shall and must sustain the love I now have for you. Love is stern, it goes where it chooses, and I thank God for it. I must close for the present, nothing more at present. My respects to all your folks. My love to you alone. Write soon. Good-by for the present, but for a short time I hope. Yours until death,

J. F. B.

Two weeks have passed, behold the change, with order much
    restored;
Our starry flag the breezes unfold where long it's been
    ignored.
The press that once proclaimed the right of states to all
    secede
Now gives to us a wholesome sheet for each and all to read.

With fervent hopes we look beyond these scenes of war and
    strife
When all these clouds shall disappear which now embitter
    life,
When all shall sing from shore to shore in one harmonious
    strain
Of peace that is lasting as the hills and free from blot or
    stain.

Go on, brave Chief, we look to you for this thrice glorious day,
When hostile bands shall be dispersed and peace again holds
    sway.
But speak the word and we'll obey, let who will, us defy;
We will plant our flag in every port where hostile colors fly.

Soon Sumpter's wall we hope to scale, displace foul treason's
    rag,
And bear aloft the starry folds of our time-honored flag.
But lead the way and we'll break in foul treason's hellish den,

And there, as here, we'll soon make way for a better class of
    men.

Or if perchance a sterner fate you prescribe, her doom
Destruction's bosom, we'll apply till there is no longer room,
Till like the walls of ancient time no stone shall hold its place
Where first foul treason bursting forth commenced its fatal
    race.

                Camped near Goldsboro, N.C., April the 9th/65

Dear Mary,

I again take the present opportunity of writing you a
few lines to inform you of good health, and hope when
this comes to hand it will find you enjoying the good and
great blessing.

I have not received but the one letter from you since
we have been here, and that is the one in answer to the
small delicate note that [I] wrote you through the month
of December while at Dalton, Ga. The reason why, I think,
is I have only had the three last ones directed to the regiment, and it has not been long enough for [me] to get
answers to them. I am satisfied you write answers to all of
mine.

Well, Mary, this is Sunday, quite a pleasant day. At
least, I should make it seem more pleasant to me if I was
in the famous town of Gilmanton. There is somebody in
that town that draws my thoughts and my attention. You
know very well now who it is. Electricity attracts lightning;
lodestone attacts steel; modesty, beauty, and mildness
attracts the attention of the mind of every man as well as
myself.

As I said, this is Sunday and a pleasant day, and what

makes it seem more pleasant, the news is such that no soldier or loyal person North or South can feel any other way than happy and grateful for the great success of our gallant army. Richmond and Petersburg are ours with twelve to fifteen thousand prisoners and several hundred cannon. Thus says an official dispatch from General Grant to General Sherman, and since we received the dispatch, report says that General Sheridan[1] has cut off the rear guard of General Lee and captured them, amounting to nearly as many as was taken at Richmond, and that the loss of the rebels in killed, wounded and prisoners is near forty-five thousand, although this last is a flying report. It may be true and it may not be true. We cannot or neither do we put much dependence in flying reports, but sometimes flying reports prove true, and I hope this one will prove true. If it does, I shall think this unholy war will soon end its wicked career, peace and union reign once more.

We have received another dispatch from Gen. Grant at twelve o'clock last night that he was pressing Lee hard, that the rebels were throwing down their arms and deserting by hundreds and that we should start after the rebel Johnston and press him to the last wall and end the rebellion, an order that General Sherman will obey as a matter of course, and our orders are to pack up and be ready to march at six o'clock tomorrow morning, with forty rounds of cartridges and six days' rations in our haversacks and thirty-five days' on wagons. This looks like a loud and vigorous campaign. I hope it will be the last one. It will probably be the last one that we will have to go through, but I hope it will be the last one for every soldier in the field, both rebel and loyal. We can whip the

[1] General Philip H. Sheridan.

rebel Gen. Johnston for we have done it more than twenty times. We had the pleasure of meeting him and whipping him quite a number of times last summer, as well as this spring and last winter. Sherman is too much for him. He beats him at his own game; every time where he thinks Billy can't come, there is where he comes every time.

Well, Mary, if I get through this tramp all right I shall have strong hopes of getting out without a scratch, but we can't tell how that will be, for many a poor fellow has filled a soldier's grave when he had but the one day to serve, some unlucky ball would take his life. This may be the case with me, but I hope not, but will trust to luck and Providence. If it is my lot to fall on the battlefield it is a great consolation to know that it was in a good and glorious cause you were engaged in.

The rebels will have to stir around now. They have lost their stronghold and will take them a long time before they get another as strong as Richmond was. I hope they never will. Grant will push them hard, as well as Sherman and many other good generals. We have no McClellans now, no generals like him [to] lay around and look at the rebels fortify for three weeks and then conclude that he can't take the place and fall back to Washington and stay there four years, but they will push them back when they meet them, fight, and disperse them.

I do not know how it will be about writing. If communications are kept open I can write. If not, this will be the last that you will hear from me for some time to come, but every time that I have a chance to write I shall write you a few lines to let you know of my whereabouts, and how I get along and how I stand the march. I expect it will go rather hard with me for awhile at first, for I have not had to march for a long time back, not enough to call or even accustom me to marching, but if I am blessed with good health I will get along very well. At least I shall call it getting along very well.

General Sherman has issued an order to fire one hundred guns from every fort along his lines. When they begin it will make the very earth tremble, as he has twenty-one forts, and will be two thousand one hundred guns fired. Just think of it in your own mind, so many cannon shots fired, as fast as they can load and fire, and you can picture it out in your own mind better than I can describe it to you.

Mary, you must and I hope you will not think if you do not get a letter from me for some time that I have forgotten you, or that I am growing cold in the love that I have pledged to you. No, never while I possess the breath of life will I grow cold, but every day brings up new hopes to me. I feel more contented now than I ever have in my life. I know that I love you better than any other on the face of this earth, and believe you can and will if you have not already returned it with the pure love that none but woman can claim to hold to as their own. Mary, perhaps you may say, why did you not apprise me of this sooner. The reason that I did not make it known to you sooner was that you were young and God knows that I would not have you take one step that you would ever regret, and the reason that I did not wait until I got home was this. I felt and knew that I was surrounded with danger every day of my life and did not know how soon I might fall a victim to the deadly aim of some rebel gun, and I felt it was my duty to inform you of my feelings toward you, and if I could be so fortunate as to have the grant of your love, it was but just and right that you should know it.

As you say, you have no doubt changed, but I know you have changed for the better. A love as strong as mine can never be forgotten. It has been cherished by me for four

long years and I shall continue to cherish it while life lasts.
I have no fears of my confidence ever being betrayed by
you. This you can see from the way that I write to you.
I know you are true. All that any or everybody could do
an[d] say would or could [not] cause me to believe any
other way. I long to see you—oh, you cannot tell how bad I
want to see you. Four months and five days, if I am
spared, my time of bondage will expire and then I hope to
meet you, worthy to receive and claim your love. It is my
desire to live for you and you only. Let others say what
they may, I know my own heart best, and if I should ever
wrong you I hope to be dealt with by the hand of the
Supreme Being who rules all things, and the just shall pre-
vail, for this is His promise. You may think strange that I
should avow my love to you in every letter, but Mary, I
know that there is one[2] there that would teach you to believe me false, and even teach you to hate and despise me
if she only does or does not know of anything serious exist-
ing between you and me. But she mistrusts it, and if I
have trifled with her feelings I am ignorant of it. She has
no reasons to think for one moment that she is or ever can
be my choice. Yet I know that she would poison your kind
and good feelings toward me with the venom of the rattlesnake. I know this and have known it for a long time. You
may wonder how I knew this. If I am spared to get back I
will tell you all. I wish you to know all my faults, but what
I am not guilty of I do not want to be accused of. I shall
have to close for once more, hoping to get a letter from
you before another week rolls around. My respects to your
folks, my love to you alone. Write soon.

Yours until death,

J. F. B. to M. E. E.

[2] Mary's Aunt Elsie.

Camped Near
Raleigh, N.C.
April the 22d/65

Dear Mary,

I again take the present opportunity of writing you a few lines to let you know of my whereabouts and how I am getting along. I am well and hope when this comes to hand it will find you enjoying the same blessing.

Well, Mary, there is plenty of news to write and all good news and I shall not attempt to write it, for you have undoubtedly heard all before this. It will go through the loyal states like wild fire. I think the long looked-[for] and hoped-for peace has come at last. We do not, or we cannot, appreciate the glorious news. Lee has surrendered the Army of Northern Virginia. Johnston has called for an armistice with views resulting to a permanent peace and the re-establishment of the laws of the Union again. We all think and believe that this cruel war has reached its end at last.

The rebel General Johnston has not surrendered yet, but he can never move again unless he cuts his way out through our lines, which would result in a great loss to him. We have him surrounded, and it is his desire to make peace. General Sherman told him he could not sign a declaration of peace, but would send to Washington to have it signed, and at the same time demanded the surrender of all the rebel troops east of the Mississippi River, which Johnston has consented to do as soon as they hear from Washington.

The soldiers on both sides are visiting back and forth all the time. We get along very well, have no trouble at all. They are willing to admit that we have whipped them, and that is all that we want of them, is to acknowledge that we are too much for them, and we will always get along very finely.

There is not a shot fired from morning until night. All is quiet and peaceable here. We are fixing up a very nice camp here to show the rebs a specimen of Yankee camp. We have planted nice small pine trees all around the camp and it is very nicely shaded, and after all it is not like home.

How we long for home now, even more than we did two months ago when everything looked dark yet. Then we expected to stay our time out. Now we expect to go home soon and are more anxious than ever to get started. We are all making up our minds what we will do as soon as we get home. Mine is and always has been at ease about that, for the first thing that I shall do will be to start up a ravine on the east side of Buffalo River to see somebody, you know who.

The worst news that we have is the loss of our President. We would all rather heard of a large defeat of some of our armies than to heard of this sad disaster, even of Sherman's army that never has known what defeat was and never will know what it is. Yet we would be willing to suffer one defeat than to have lost our good, honest, and patriotic President, Abraham Lincoln.

Our army, that is, the army of Sherman, has been successful in every move that it has made since the commencement of this war, and we believe it always will be, with Sherman to command it.

The weather is very pleasant and warm. Everything looks pleasant, too pleasant to be wearing life away in this lonely place. We have a very pleasant place for a camp, and have everything comfortable as can be in camp life, and after all it is a disagreeable life to live, no society, no good times, only what we can get up in the way of stories, and they have become old long ago. We all hope there is a better time coming now, and soon. [The] human mind is never easy, always longing for something new. Home and its pleasures and endearments are all our thoughts now, all our talk, and all our desire.

General Sherman comes around to see us occasionally. He tells us he hopes to soon march one of the best armies in the world home in a few days. The first of May is the day set now to start for Washington. [*Rest of letter missing.*]

>   In Camp Near
>   Richmond, Va.
>   May the 11th/65

Dear Mary,

I received your more then welcome letter of April the 28th and was very glad to hear from you once more and to hear that you were well at the time of writing. I am well and hearty, never was in better health than at the present time. Hope you still enjoy the good blessing of health.

The letter that I received had 18 stamps enclosed in it, and you spoke of writing one previous to that one and sending more stamps in it, but I have not received it and am sorry you sent so many. My intention was for you to use part of them yourself. I will probably get the letter before long as it has probably gone to N.C. and will have to follow me back here, but it will be read with interest when it comes to hand.

I have been waiting very patiently to get a letter from you since I arrived here, and it has come at last, been read, and soon will be answered. I wrote to you every opportunity that presented itself up to the time of Johnston's surrender, which I wrote you in my last. There was a misunderstanding of the terms of surrender and we had to start after the rebel line. We sent in lead and iron for a few moments with too much effect for him to stand long, so he came to our terms and we marched back to our old camp, being gone only three days.

Washed up and prepared for a march to Richmond, and what we call a homeward march. We arrived at this place day before yesterday, the 9th of May, and tomorrow, the 12th, we start for Washington. The weather is very warm and many of the men melted on the march up here. Some fell dead in the road, some died soon after, and some are getting well. We have one hundred and thirty miles to march; then I hope our marching will be through. I think we have done enough of the business.

I have been over in the city taking a view of Libby Prison and Belle Island. They are gloomy looking places for men to live, but our prisoners were well acquainted with both places. Richmond is a very fine place. It is a large city.

There is not much news to write and if there was I could not think of any, for all we think of now is home, sweet home, and the ones most dear to us.

Some think we will be at home to spend the Fourth of July. I hope we will, but am afraid we will not for everything works so slow in the army. At the same time, I cannot see why we cannot get home by that time. But thank fortune the war is over, and the prospects are that we will get home sometime sooner or later, one or the other, the former I hope.

We feel as though we were going out of the wilderness, our Moses at the head of the columns, his name is Sherman. He can and will lead us through, all safe and sound. He has done it so far and we are all willing to trust to him yet.

The boys are all talking about Mexico, all are bound for Mexico, but I have got enough of soldiering to last me for the present. I understand they are recruiting very fast in the city of New York for that purpose. As for myself, I am willing to stake my life for my own country but not for any other. Let those go that choose, but not me. The Mexicans are offering very large pay to our men to induce them to go, and there is a large number in this army that will go. At least they say they will as soon as they get out of this. I believe that I can enjoy myself without Mexican gold. Our greenbacks are good enough for me at present.

Well, Mary, there is a rainstorm coming up, and I shall have to hurry with my letter or I shall miss getting it off. The boys are all well as usual. Andrew Lunderville was up to my Co. talking with me when I received your letter. Gave him your respects as you desired. Dan and Pratt are well and hearty. [*Rest of letter missing.*]

CHAPTER EIGHT

May 1865–June 1865

"Our country is safe"

By the 23rd of May, 1865, the men in Sherman's Army of the Tennessee had reached the outskirts of Washington, D.C. Here they encamped, across the river from the famed Army of the Potomac, for whom they had no particular affection. Technically, the two armies had been allied in a common cause for the past four years, but that formal relationship had produced no feeling of brotherhood between them. In fact, the Union soldiers from the west usually got along better personally with Confederate soldiers than they did with their fellow Union soldiers from the east. Fortunately, the war was over before they were all brought together at Washington, D.C. The fierce competition between eastern and western armies regarding the number of battles fought and won had now come to an end, and there was a spirit of reconciliation in the air.

On May 24, 1865, John Brobst and his regiment proudly participated in the Grand Review of Union troops in Washington.[1] The once unkempt and undisciplined western volunteers were now on their best behavior. Sixty-five thousand strong, Sherman's veterans marched down Pennsylvania Avenue in perfect order. They wanted to show their Sherman and the world that they knew how to march if they cared to. It was a stirring spectacle and a memorable experience both for the troops and for General Sherman—a climax to the whole network of events which had combined to carve these veteran infantry soldiers out of farmers and backwoodsmen.

The desire to return home was now almost too much for John to bear. The infantry had become a familiar way of life, and he would miss the comradeship and close friends he had found here. But he knew that army life would not do as a career for him; it would have to be just a brief, unforgettable episode in an otherwise ordinary life as a frontier farmer. And so Private John Brobst waited impatiently, but with mixed feelings, for the final order which would enable him to return once more to Gilmanton and his Mary.

[1] See the account of this parade in Grant, *Personal Memoirs,* II, 534–35; Sherman's account in Miers, *The General Who Marched to Hell,* p. 325.

Camp Near
Washington, D.C.,
May the 27th/65

Dear Mary,

I received yours of the 4th of May and it was read with much pleasure as all of your letters are that are received by me. I was glad to hear that your health was good and hope it will remain so. My health is very good and has been since my return to the regt.

Well, Mary, the best news that I can hear is there are some prospects of our getting home sometime during the summer, but how soon or how long it will be before we get on the way [I can not tell]. I hope not long, as we are all anxious to see home and friends and those that are dearer to us than friends can be. Home, how sweet that name sounds in the ear of a soldier. How every soldier longs for that place nearer to heaven than any other on earth called home. How rightfully may the poet say, "Home sweet, sweet home. There is no place like home, let it be ever so humble. There is no place like home." And yet if there was no one there to make home dear, it would be as all other places of pleasure, merely the impulses of a moment and all then would be forgotten.

As for me, I thank the Almighty that there is one to make home a sweet place of repose for me, that there is one in this world that I can place all my confidence and affections on and have no mistrustful thoughts in regard to it, and all my hopes hover around that one. I can settle down there as willingly as the bird with its weary wings settles down in soft repose in its ever-welcome nest. The mind of mortal man is never easy until it has an object to place all its confidence and affections on. Then comes contentment, and not before this can the mind of any human being become familiar with contentment. I know this from experience. I have seen many that I could respect and see a great many good qualities in their character, but still there seemed to be something lacking, something that did not please me.

Never did I see any person until I saw you that I could convince myself that I did or could or ever had a desire to love. And how often have I sat and argued in my own mind to satisfy myself that I did love you, for I really had gone so far as to believe that I was not capable of loving anyone, but you have taught me different. You have taught me to believe and know that I can love when the right one comes in view.

Mary, you say you long to see me. You can rest assured that I also long to see you. You occupy my thoughts more than any other in this world and you always shall. Let come what may, still you have my love. I claim you as mine in the sight of God. Even if some other pleased you better than me, and discard me, yet I should claim you, for God has created a mate for all and no other can ever be mine.

I hope we will get home in time to spend the Fourth of July at home. How pleasant next Fourth will be, with peace as we may say throughout our much-loved land. All can enjoy themselves much better knowing that our glorious old flag demands respect from all, and compels all to pay reverence to it. We have no more fears or doubts as to how this rebellion will terminate. Our country is surely safe now. There is not a doubt in regard to the ability of our great and good government to crush all rebellions that may spring up through petty politicians and fire eaters.

Jeff Davis has found the last ditch that he was going to

die in, and it is not far from Fort Monroe, and I think it
will not be long until the dying part comes. He must feel
gay. I think I should if I was in his place.

You have probably heard all the particulars connected
with his capture and I will not write them. There are all
kinds of pictures, representing his capture, in the city of
Washington. He is certainly the greatest nuisance the
world ever produced. He is not fit to live and he certainly
is not fit to die, but he must go up some ten feet above the
face of the earth and perform on a tight rope for the bene-
fit of a society called the Loyal People of America. We
have no doubt but what there are some of Jefferson's good
friends that feel sorry for him, those in the North I refer to,
and probably would be willing to share his fate if they
were not such contemptible cowards, for every man that
sympathized with the rebellion in the North are cowards,
and we have more respect for those that actually took
up arms against us and showed themselves men and not
cowards, than we can of sneaking, low-lived, miserable
cowards. I refer to those that have cried our cause down
at our backs, and at our faces the soldier was a very fine
fellow. God hates a coward, and why not man hate one,
when the ruler of all things despises them poor outcasts
from heaven and earth, and not fit to be styled American
citizens.

Well, Mary, there is not much news to write, for we are
not foraging and living off the fat of the land of the lovely
South, but we are on the banks of the famed river Potomac, the place that derives its note from grand reviews
of the Grand Army of the Potomac. We used to get the
news that General Meade[2] had crossed the famous river

[2] General George G. Meade.

Rapidan, with seven days rations bound for Richmond. We can look for stirring news from that quarter soon.— Three days later. Grand review of the Army of the Potomac, grand condition of the army, general good feeling exists, all confidence placed in the ability of General Mead.—Still three days later. General Meade recrosses the Rapidan. All quiet on the Potomac, except now and then light picket firing.

But this is played out, I hope, for Richmond is gone up the spout, and the Army of the Potomac has the name of one city on its banner, while we have the names of seventeen. But all praise is due to the Army of the Potomac, for it has always done all it has been ordered to do, and it could do no more. If they will keep still, we will not poke fun at them, and if they do not, we will poke fun at them.

The Governor of Wis.[3] was here and made us a very nice, good speech. He says the 25th has the brightest name on the record of the state.

We had a grand review of Sherman's army the other day, and it is admitted that Sherman's vandals did better and made a better appearance than the famed Army of the Potomac. We all feel well. Sherman's enemies that attempted to cry are taking it all back. Sherman is the best man in the United States, and every man in his army thinks the same.

It has been raining for two days and nights and is raining yet, and the prospects is we will have a little rain if it keeps on.

Dan has just got a letter from his Sheboygan Duck, and he is light as a feather. He can hardly keep himself on the ground. She filled two foolscaps sheets of paper full, and I

[3] Governor James T. Lewis.

do not know but two fools' caps that was not paper. All
fun, you know. He is well, Thompson is well, the boys are
all well but the recruits, and they are well bodily but
heartsick. They have to stay in the army. It makes them
feel for home, but their three hundred dollars bounty will
not let them reach home yet for a while. Too bad, poor
fellows.

Give my respects to all your folks and all who you see fit
to give.

Write soon, Co. G, 25th Wis. Vol., D.C. Nothing more
at present. Good-by. My love to yourself. Yours until
death,

John F. Brobst
Mary E. Englesby

Camped Near
Washington, D.C.
June the 2d/65

Dear Mary,

I was more than glad to receive another welcome mes-
senger from you and hear that your health was good, and
your mind firm and steadfast on the subject that is of most
interest to me and my welfare and future happiness. You
cannot appreciate the regard and respect that I have for
you and how anxious I watch for the mail and look for the
postmark on the letter when it is my good fortune to receive one. Letters, how sweet that sound echoes through
the ears of the absent ones. No other is a greater or better
blessing than that of letter writing, to know that we can
hear from those we cannot see, and better still to know

that they are penned by the hand of those we love. How miserable all would be if it was not for this one good science, the art of writing. We can hear and know the feelings of the absent as well as of those that are present.

My health is very good. We are rolling in the dirt, waiting with all the patience that we can muster up for the happy hour to come when President Johnson will say, "Arise and depart, thou good and faithful servants of your country, for your work is done, and well done. Go to your homes and loved ones. There remain and do yourselves honor there as good citizens to the cause that you have risked your lives and fought so well and long to maintain." A few more days of patience will, I hope, end the great suspense that we are laboring under at present. We will soon go home, that we all know, but oh, how slow the days and hours pass away. How we long at night for the morning to come, and in the morning for night to come, wishing ourselves near eternity day after day, all for the sake of home and its endearments and to see those we love and respect. Three long years of complete banishment as we might say from all society that is modest and good. When we think of it we are all willing to admit that it is not unjust to long for the future. Perhaps it will give less pleasure to some than the adventures and rudeness of a soldier's life, but as for myself, I think with the bright prospects that are now before me that a home in the far west, a peaceable home in the cold and fleecy regions of the snowy north will be more preferable than the adventure of a soldier's life in the sunny south.

Yesterday was a day of humiliation and prayer through the United States. I was down in the city of Washington. It looked very sad and lonely. Everything was bedecked with crepe in mourning for our much-loved and respected

President, Abraham Lincoln. He was given to us to do the great work that was before us to do. He has done it well, with a good, pure and forgiving heart, and when the day began to dawn in the far east, noble man he was called to go. To the fate of an over-ruling Providence we meekly but sorrowfully bow. How much better all the South would have fared if they had not taken the life of the best friend they had in this wide world, and to take his life in such a base and cowardly a manner. They have slain Mercy, and now they must abide by the sterner master, Justice. The man they have to deal with now is a great and I believe a good man, and one that will deal out justice to every leader of treason in the South, and to all of the vile villains that instigated and executed the horrid schemes of the death of President Lincoln. He has more than one hundred of them confined in the capital prison now, and has men all over the country searching for more. I hope he will succeed in capturing every one of them and hang every one that had the least thing to do in the plot.

Jeff Davis is here in the city of Washington to await his trial. He was brought up here on the 30th of May. He is on board one of the Monitors near the Navy yard. The boat does not come near the shore. They are determined that he will never make his escape, and all the loyal people are glad that there is so much precaution taken in his welfare. I have not seen him, but he must feel well to visit the old capital once more. No doubt he would feel better if it was under almost any other circumstances.

The boys are getting up all kinds of tricks to pass away time—suing one another, having regular lawsuits, sworn witnesses, have our lawyers, judges, juries, and all in good style. They are going to have a great lawsuit with me this afternoon.

When I came up from town yesterday, one of the boys that was on guard gave me a paper to give to his tent mate. I brought the paper up to camp and concluded the freight on the paper was worth the first chance of reading it, and did so. Then I told them that, that is William Doughty[4] and the others, that Mr. DeGroff[5] had sent the paper to them, but as freight was rather high and as I never expected to get any other pay, I kept the paper until I read the news. So when Mr. DeGroff came to camp they apprised him of my conduct, and he has sued me for breach of trust and claims damage, as I did not get through with the paper until dark, and they had to burn candles to read the news, and they are going to make me pay for the candles.

We do the business up in regular style. It would make you laugh to hear some of our lawsuits.

You said that Mrs. and Miss Wilcox went to Alma to meet Wallace. I wonder if it was a happy meeting. I think it must have been very agreeable to both parties. The inconvenience that I can see in such a meeting is the distance between the two parties. I should [think] they need strong lungs to talk so as to be heard the distance they had between them. But after all, it was too bad to be disappointed, but they will have to learn that they cannot expect to meet anyone at Alma unless they stay there all the time, for we may all be there in one week and we may not be there for two months. This military law lets men go when others get ready to let them go. It is not as we say, but as others say.

[4] Corporal William J. Doughty, Maxville, Wisconsin, Company G, 25th Wisconsin Infantry Regiment.

[5] Allen and John DeGroff, Maxville, Wisconsin, were both in Company G, 25th Wisconsin Regiment.

Well, they are calling on me to appear at court to attend
to my suit, but I shall keep on writing until I get through,
and then we will see what their sentence will be, and I
will write what the fine or damage will be. We have to pay
all fines very prompt, pay the lawyer and the witness, just
the same as if we had a real lawsuit at home or any other
place.

Your schoolteacher is quite a young girl. I should think
she is not but a very little older than you are. You would
be rather a large scholar for her to punish, but I know you
will not need any punishment. I used to like to go to
school to young schoolma'ms; then when I did anything
wrong I could tell them how I loved them and as a matter
of course they could not punish one that they know loves
them, and in that way I could get clear of a great many of
my bad capers at school. Perhaps you could do the same
if it was a young man, but I do not know how it would
work, the teacher being a young lady. I will be up there
soon to wake some of you up if you want talk and noise to
make time pass off. I think I can suit all.

George Gilkey[6] was over here to see us the other day.
He stayed all night with us. He feels sick as well as all of
the soldiers that have not been in but a short time, as they
all have to stay and look at the others feel good and see
them start for home.

I think Haldon[7] will have his hands full if them secesh
girls are as big devils where he is as they have been where
I have been. They are most always cross as they can live,
but all say the Yankees are the best looking, and they
would like them very well if they were not so tormented

[6] Sergeant George W. Gilkey, Gilmanton, Wisconsin, Company
K, 36th Wisconsin Infantry Regiment.
[7] Mary's uncle, Haldon Englesby.

mean and drive their brothers and sweethearts away from
their homes. It is too bad, but General Sherman tells us
to do so, and anything he tells us to do we are bound to
do, but he has left us.

He gave us his farewell address yesterday. We are sorry
to see our leader leave us, but we cannot be together always. His speech was short but very good. Told us of the
hardships we have passed through and how well we did it.
He is worshipped by all of his army. We know he thinks
himself no better than the common soldier. He takes another command on the Ohio River. He takes most of his
troops with him, only [except] those that [are] going
home. They say we will start for home one week from tomorrow. I do not know how true it is.

Well, Mary, I suppose the town of Gilmanton is settled
up so much since I have been there that I can hardly find
out where I want to go. I think I know where I want to go
first, and I think with a good pocket compass I can find
the way. I know where the house stands. It stands at the
head of a ravine, and the road runs along the bottom of
the ravine. I remember of going to the house once for
rattlesnake oil and found another gent there, and told him
I should have to fight a duplicate as I thought that much
better than to fight a duel.

You say you wish you could write as long letters as I
can. You can if you would think of as much nonsense as I
do, for I believe I could write all day and there would not
be as much in it as some could get on a half sheet of paper.
I love to get letters from you, short or long; the long ones
are the most acceptable in one respect, but either is very
acceptable. Short ones are better than none, and I suppose
there is nothing going on up there to write about.

Well, Mary, I have lost the great lawsuit for nonappearance. They got a judgment against me for the amount of one cent to be paid in bread and butter, and the cost all summed up amounts to half a cent to be paid in whiskey, and must be paid inside of one week or I am to be cast into prison for the space of fifteen moments and be fed on bread and water. Rather a hard sentence I think, don't you?

Well, as I am afraid your patience will be nearly exhausted by the time you read this, I think I shall have to close for this time, hoping to meet you soon and never to part again until death shall part us. You say you are mine forever. Ten thousand thanks to you, and I hope to prove myself worthy of so noble a prize. Give my respects to all who you choose.

When you write, direct to Madison, Wis. and do not put this on: 2nd Brig., 1st Div., 17th A.C., but just this: Co. G, 25 regt., Wis. Vol.

Good-by for the present. Yours in undying and unchangeable love,

John F. Brobst

Historical Note

Private John Brobst was officially mustered out of the Union Army at Washington, D.C., on June 7, 1865. He and his comrades of the Twenty-fifth Wisconsin Volunteers immediately began the long trip back to Wisconsin by train and riverboat and arrived in Madison on June 11, 1865. From there it was but a day's journey by rail and wagon to Gilmanton, where John was welcomed as a hero. He was one of the fortunate ones, as nearly half of the thousand men in his regiment did not live to return to their homes.

John kept his promise to Mary, and they were married

six months after his return to Gilmanton, just before her sixteenth birthday. John and Mary had a long and happy married life. They raised three children and lived to celebrate their golden wedding anniversary in 1915. John was a farmer and stock buyer, and is remembered by Ira Britton, a lifelong resident of Gilmanton, as being instrumental in bringing the first telephone line to that village. John and Mary later moved to Mondovi, a few miles from Gilmanton, and it was there that they spent their last years. John died in 1917 at the age of seventy-eight. Mary died twenty-six years later, at the age of ninety-three, having outlived two of her three children.

Mary Brobst is still remembered as Grandma or Great-grandma by many relatives and former neighbors in Mondovi. Her own particular philosophy of life, which guided her through long years of both happiness and sorrow, was stated often and pointedly: "It's so to be."

One small item of interest might be added here. Although she had married John out of love and of her own free will, there was one other person who still shared Mary's affections. This came to light when she gave a pair of vases to one of her grandchildren, just a few years before her death. She said then that the vases had been a wedding gift from Dan Hadley, and that she had never told John where they came from.

Some of Mary and John's grandchildren are now grandparents themselves, but still remember being told countless tales of battles, marches, prisons, and rebs by their grandfather. He had served the Union well and willingly at a time when its very existence was threatened, and he never begrudged the years or effort he had spent in helping to secure the future of his country.

Bibliography, Index

Bibliography

Abernethy, Byron R. (ed.). *Private Elisha Stockwell, Jr., Sees the Civil War*. Norman, Oklahoma, 1958.

Campbell, Henry C. *Wisconsin in Three Centuries, 1634–1905*. New York, 1906. Vol. III.

Catton, Bruce. *This Hallowed Ground: The Story of the Union Side of the Civil War*. New York, 1956.

Clark, James I. *Chronicles of Wisconsin*. Madison, 1955.

Commager, Henry Steele (ed.). *The Blue and the Gray: The Story of the Civil War as Told by Participants*. Indianapolis, 1950. Vol. II.

Cooke, Chauncey H. "Badger Boy in Blue: The Letters of Chauncey H. Cooke," *Wisconsin Magazine of History*, IV (1920–1921), 75–100, 208–17, 322–44, 431–56; V (1921–1922), 63–98.

Dowdey, Clifford. *Experiment in Rebellion*. New York, 1946.

Grant, U. S. *Personal Memoirs of U. S. Grant*. New York, 1885.

Hinkley, Julian W. *A Narrative of Service with the Third Wisconsin Infantry*. Madison, 1912.

Johnson, Robert U., and Clarence C. Buell (eds.). *Battles and Leaders of the Civil War*. New York, 1887. Vols. III and IV.

Love, William De Loss. *Wisconsin in the War of the Rebellion*. Chicago, 1866.

Miers, Earl Schenk. *The General Who Marched to Hell*. New York, 1951.

Pratt, Fletcher. *Civil War in Pictures*. New York, 1955.

Quiner, E. B. *The Military History of Wisconsin*. Chicago, 1866.

Rhodes, James Ford. *History of the Civil War, 1861–1865*. New York, 1917.

Roesch, Philip. "Memorandum of Philip Roesch, Co. H, 25th Reg., Wisconsin Volunteers, Kept All During His Service." Typewritten copy in possession of Wisconsin Historical Society, Madison.

Street, James. *The Civil War: An Unvarnished Account of the Late but Still Lively Hostilities*. New York, 1953.

Thwaites, Reuben G. *Wisconsin: The Americanization of a French Settlement*. Boston, 1908.

———, Asa C. Tilton, and Frederick Merk (eds.). *Civil War Messages and Proclamations of Wisconsin War Governors*. Madison, 1912.

Wescott, M. Ebenezer. *Civil War Letters, 1861 to 1865, Written by a Boy in Blue to His Mother*. [Mora? Minn.], 1909.

Wiley, Bell Irvin. *The Life of Billy Yank, the Common Soldier of the Union*. Indianapolis, 1951.

Wisconsin. Adjutant General's Office. *Annual Report of the Adjutant General for 1865*. Madison, 1912.

———. *Roster of Wisconsin Volunteers, War of the Rebellion, 1861–1865*. Madison, 1886. Vol. II.

Index